THE
REGENERATION
HANDBOOK

Praise for *The Regeneration Handbook*

This is a handbook for millions of us who have not given up on restoring health, sanity, vitality, and a higher moral purpose to our world—even with the dangerous head winds. It is a glossary of relevant ideas for regeneration activists. It is a compendium of projects that have worked. Don provides an analysis of where the movements for regeneration are, and what next steps can be. He is the kind of leader we need.

> — Vicki Robin, author, *Your Money or Your Life* and *Blessing the Hands that Feed Us*, and host, What Could Possibly Go Right?

Born from his years of experience in numerous and different roles, synthesized from his clarity of where we are, and offered from a compassionate and wise heart, Don has written a true field guide for stepping forward to serve this time. Let us use this very practical guide and see what's possible, embodying Václav Havel's definition of hope: "Not the conviction that something will turn out well, but the certainty that something is worth doing no matter how it turns out."

> — Dr. Margaret Wheatley, author, *Restoring Sanity* and *So Far from Home*

If you want to build a future that extends beyond the polycrisis currently gripping humanity, then regeneration should be your key search word. And your search lands here. This is the book to inform your personal and communitarian efforts as humans cease being fossil fools and transition into wise Earth stewards.

> — Richard Heinberg, author, *Power: Limits and Prospects for Humans Survival* and Senior Fellow, Post Carbon Institute

Weaving together personal transformation, community organizing, and new economic thinking, this handbook is chock-full of insights from Don Hall's lifetime commitment to the great work of our time—healing the collateral damage of economic growth and globalization.

> — Woody Tasch, founder, Slow Money Institute and beetcoin.org

Full of keen analysis and deep feeling, *The Regeneration Handbook* is an important reflection on our predicament as a species, and both the challenges and opportunities our movements face in transforming global human society. If we are to have any hope, it requires being real about what we're dealing with. Don Hall has brought us both.

> — Sky Blue, former executive director and board member, Foundation for Intentional Community

The environmental, social, and economic polycrisis is ending the world as we know it. But that's not necessarily a bad thing. In *The Regeneration Handbook*, Don Hall illustrates how the great transition could be a bane, or if we look at it as a unique opportunity for transformation, it could be a boon. Whether it is one or the other is up to all of us. Shared challenges demand shared solutions!

—Tom Llewellyn, executive director, Shareable

Many things about our future are murky—but one thing is clear, and that is that a rapidly changing planet is going to demand some rapid changes from all of us, in our communities and in our own selves. This book is a darned good place to start thinking through those transitions.

— Bill McKibben, author, *The End of Nature*

If you're feeling hopeless about our future, you've found the right antidote! With *The Regeneration Handbook*, Don Hall has done a brilliant job summing up the past couple decades of thinking on regenerative social change, and has written a clear, inspiring, and entertaining call to action.

— Adam Brock, organizational ecologist, Regenerate Change, and author, *Change Here Now: Permaculture Solutions for Personal and Community Transformation*

If there is one book that at least a billion of us must read at this crossroads of human civilization, it's Don Hall's *The Regeneration Handbook*. It's powerful. It's lyrical. Dip into it wherever you like. Almost every paragraph is potent and memorable. It's deeply motivating in a way that you may not be able to resist. Don debunks the ideas that it's too late, that humanity is irredeemably lazy or selfish, or indeed that we are the doomed pinnacle of human evolution. A kinder, wiser, more humble, and much more meaningful civilization awaits— for all of us who decide to go there. Your choice.

— Dr. Phoebe Barnard, scientist and professor, and co-founder, Global Restoration Collaborative

The Regeneration Handbook distills authenticity. It explores with care and detail the transition principles and the movement, including the author's personal process, to inspire you to act. An essential book in this time of uncertainty and needed regeneration. It will surely support you through your own evolutionary journey.

— Juan del Río, co-founder, Transition Spain, and film co-director, *Alter Nativas: Building Possible Futures*

THE REGENERATION HANDBOOK

TRANSFORM YOURSELF
TO TRANSFORM
THE WORLD

DON HALL

new society
PUBLISHERS

Cover design by Diane McIntosh.
Cover image: base images © iStock, composite by Diane McIntosh.
Illustrations by Carrie Van Horn.

Printed in Canada. First printing June, 2024.

Inquiries regarding requests to reprint all or part of *The Regeneration Handbook* should be addressed to New Society Publishers at the address below. To order directly from the publishers, please call 250-247-9737 or order online at www.newsociety.com.

Any other inquiries can be directed by mail to:

New Society Publishers
P.O. Box 189, Gabriola Island, BC V0R 1X0, Canada
(250) 247-9737

LIBRARY AND ARCHIVES CANADA CATALOGUING IN PUBLICATION

Title: The regeneration handbook : transform yourself to transform the world / Don Hall.

Names: Hall, Don, author.

Description: Includes bibliographical references and index.

Identifiers: Canadiana (print) 20240302052 | Canadiana (ebook) 20240302125 | ISBN 9780865719958 (softcover) | ISBN 9781771423847 (EPUB) | ISBN 9781550927887 (PDF)

Subjects: LCSH: Social change. | LCSH: Activism. | LCSH: Leadership.

Classification: LCC HM831.H35 2024 | DDC 303.4—dc23

New Society Publishers' mission is to publish books that contribute in fundamental ways to building an ecologically sustainable and just society, and to do so with the least possible impact on the environment, in a manner that models this vision.

Dedication

First and foremost, I want to dedicate *The Regeneration Handbook* to my teachers, mentors, and predecessors on this path. You blazed the trail and led the way. Your words and actions echo far across space and time, providing abundant inspiration, encouragement, and guidance. Without you, I would surely be lost and this book wouldn't exist.

I also want to dedicate *The Regeneration Handbook* to all of my friends and colleagues who have devoted their lives to bringing about a truly just, sustainable, and regenerative future. I applaud your courage, compassion, creativity, and persistence. I know how deeply challenging this work can be. Although it may sometimes seem as if our efforts aren't fully appreciated and couldn't possibly matter in the grand scheme of things, nothing we do is ever lost. Together, we are weaving a vast underground mycelial network, just waiting for the right conditions to burst forth.

Finally, *The Regeneration Handbook* is dedicated to everyone who longs for a better world, believes it's still possible, and wants to learn how to help. You are my greatest hope for the future. I trust this book will reward your time and attention with many valuable perspectives, insights, tools, practices, and resources that will enable you to live into your deepest calling and experience the profound fulfillment that brings.

Contents

Foreword

It is a joy to be asked to write a foreword for this delightful book. Having written most of the early published books about Transition, it is to be greatly celebrated that other voices are now stepping in and sharing their insights, learnings, and perspectives on Transition concepts, and hopefully there will be many more. To name just four highly different publications from the past decade, there's Luigi Russi's brilliant *Everything Gardens* (2015), a deeply insightful case study of Transition in practice in one single community (my town of Totnes), and *Reliance* (2023) by Elie Wattelet, Michel Maxime Egger, and Tylie Grosjean, currently only available in French, which is a thorough guide to what will become familiar to you in this book as "Inner Transition." There's also *The Essential Guide to Doing Transition*, a free resource published by Transition Network, now available in 17 different languages, which attempts to distill, from the experience of Transition groups around the world, everything you need to know to begin this journey wherever you are.

And then, from the world of fiction, there was David Nobbs, the famous British comedy writer, who in 2014 wrote *The Secret Life of Sally Mottram*, a beautiful and hilarious novel about the eponymous heroine's attempts to bring the Transition movement to her town, having picked up some books about Transition while on holiday. These and other titles reflect the wider sense of ownership of this movement and its ideas, and of how, as Luigi Russi argued, Transition ought not be talked about as a *movement*, as academics who so love something they can pin down and put under a microscope tend to think of it, but as a *moving*.

By this, Russi means this movement's adaptation, its "multi-dimensionality," its playfulness, creativity, and openness to new ideas; its influences and practices, which together sit at the heart of what Transition is about, rather than the models published in those early books and resources representing little more than snapshots of a handful of people's interpretation of how it looked at that particular moment. I have always loved the willingness in Transition to throw the whole model up in the air and to be constantly reassessing what it is and how it works. The French artist Jean Dubuffet once wrote "Art doesn't go to sleep in the bed made for it. It would sooner run away than say its own name: what it likes is to be incognito. Its best moments are when it forgets what it's called." I feel the same about Transition.

Some people have asked, for example, for a "revised and updated" version of *The Transition Handbook*, the first book on the subject published in 2008. But at this point in time, who would write it? How could it possibly capture the sheer extent and diversity of voices and ideas within this movement? It would be quite the logistical challenge! And yet the book that you are holding in your hands takes a wide, systems-level overview of the contribution the Transition movement can make, and positions it in the wider movements for climate and social justice.

As someone who has been a Transition practitioner at a local level (Transition Sarasota), a regional level (Transition Colorado), and a national level (Transition US), Don Hall is in the perfect position to write this book. It emerges from hard-won experience. I know from personal experience the blood, sweat, and tears that it can take to amass the experience that is shared in this book. This is no armchair exercise, some review of the academic literature—this is a book written from the frontlines, a pulling together of learning and insights, from things that didn't work as much as from things that did. Creating successful Transition groups is not easy, but one of the beauties of the Transition movement is that people often share what works as much as they share what doesn't. Insights from the experiences Don shares here, his own and that of the wider movement, will make it so much easier for you to get started.

One of the things I notice in my own work as someone who writes, whether about Transition, imagination, or the need for positive future visions combined with determined action, is that sometimes ideas I put out into the world get picked up, and sometimes they don't. Sometimes people will come up to me after a talk and say they were disappointed that a joke or a graphic or a story that I used in talks seven years ago aren't still there.

There is something about being curious and inquisitive and not wanting to be like a band that always plays the same songs, that means I keep moving forward and not getting bored of the sound of my own voice!

But it is delightful to see that the "Five Stages" model from *The Transition Companion*—still my favorite book about Transition and yet the one that sold the least copies and was never translated into other languages—was picked up like a ruby from long weeds by Don, here.

Inspired by Christopher Alexander's classic *A Pattern Language*, still the one book I would take to a desert island, *The Transition Companion* reimagined Transition as a pantry full of ingredients, each ingredient something we had seen working for Transition groups. And yet, we argued, there are also stages to this, in the same way Alexander did when reflecting on how cities are designed and planned.

There are the ingredients we need when we start, the ingredients we need when our initiative is building up a head of steam, the ingredients that allow us to dream of what could be. It's a joy to see those stages woven into this book and that they are felt to be a useful tool.

Political theorist Wendy Brown recently said in an interview with *The Nation*, "only a compelling vision of a less frightening and insecure future will recruit anyone to a progressive or revolutionary alternative future—or rouse apolitical citizens for the project of making that future. This vision must be seductive and exciting, and it must be embodied in seductive and exciting leadership and movements, hopefully oriented by an ethic of responsibility." That's what I increasingly see as one of the key roles of Transition, to speak to the future we could still create, to bring it alive for people, and to then be one of the movements that takes people's hands and says "come on, let's do this, it's not so hard." It is this combination of imagination and practical action, so powerfully captured in this book, that echoes the words of prison abolitionist Mariame Kaba: "we must imagine while we build. Always both."

Climate scientist and activist Peter Kalmus was once asked what gives him hope. His response was beautiful: "the fact that we've barely tried yet." It's not like we don't know what to do. The "seductive and exciting leadership and movements" Brown speaks of are what Don sets out here, as is her call that "this vision must be seductive and exciting." "Seductive" is a beautiful word in the context of *The Regeneration Handbook*. How can we most skillfully make community mobilization feel seductive in a way that filters upwards, impacting local, regional, and then national government?

There are so many brilliant ideas and tried-and-tested tools in this book. It is a treasure house of riches by which you might turn your concern for this beautiful planet, your rage at what's been done to it, to its people, and to the creatures we share it with, into practical, impactful action, while all the time building a culture in your group(s) whereby you look after each other and design for the long haul. And yes, when they're all pulled together as Don has done here, they do offer a seductive vision of where we go from here. Let's get to it.

— Rob Hopkins, founder of the Transition movement and
author of several books, including most recently
*From What Is to What If: Unleashing the Power
of Imagination to Create the Future We Want*

Introduction

We humans appear on the cosmic calendar so recently that our recorded history occupies only the last few seconds of the last minutes of December 31st. We are the legacy of 15 billion years of cosmic evolution. We have a choice: we can enhance life and come to know the universe that made us, or we can squander our 15-billion-year heritage in meaningless self-destruction.

— Carl Sagan, *Cosmos*[1]

We live in extraordinary times. We all know this on some level, but typically take it for granted as we go about our daily lives. As a result, far too many of us continue to merely cycle through our status quo routines as our world careens ever closer to disaster. However, if we can embrace our global predicament as the opportunity for unprecedented transformation it is, it can act as a catalyst for us to unlock our full potential and leave behind a legacy we can be proud of.

According to the current scientific consensus, our universe emerged out of unfathomable mystery in the Big Bang 13.8 billion years ago. Dispersed particles gradually self-organized into atoms, which joined to make more complex molecules, which eventually coalesced into stars, planets, and galaxies. Earth itself formed approximately 4.5 billion years ago, and fossilized microbes have been found in hydrothermal ocean vents dating back 3.5 billion years, providing the earliest evidence of life.

In comparison, the emergence of *Homo sapiens* 300,000 years ago could be considered an extremely recent phenomenon. For 97 percent of our history, humans have overwhelmingly lived in small, tight-knit communities, nomadically hunting and gathering in relative symbiosis with the Earth. It's only been within the last 10,000 years since the Agricultural Revolution that we've increasingly settled in towns and cities apart from nature, enclosed and divided up the commons, and developed complex hierarchies to control surplus resources and labor.

While this process of expansion based on the subjugation of nature and Indigenous peoples has continued ever since, what we think of as modern civilization really only dates back about 260 years to the beginning of the fossil-fueled Industrial Revolution. At that time, global population stood at 600 million. There were no cars, planes, trucks, buses, or trains; no telephones, radios, TVs, or computers; no supermarkets or big-box stores filled with cheap goods and produce from all over the world; no electricity, air conditioning, or curbside trash collection; no plastic bags or pharmaceuticals; no rock concerts, blockbuster movies, or professional sports; no health insurance, paid vacations, or retirement plans.

Despite our current way of life having only existed for less than 0.1% of human history, we tend to think it's normal and assume it will continue indefinitely because it's all we've ever known. However, exponential growth in human population, consumption of natural resources, and greenhouse gas emissions over the past two and a half centuries has already pushed our planet to its breaking point, ushering in what geologists have termed the

Figure 1.1. Evolutionary timeline of the universe, Earth, and humanity.

Event	Years Ago	Percentage of Cosmic Time
Birth of the Universe	13.8 billion	100%
Formation of Earth	4.5 billion	33%
Emergence of Life	3.5 billion	25%
Emergence of *Homo sapiens*	300,000	0.002%
Agricultural Revolution	10,000	0.00007%
Industrial Revolution	260	0.000002%

"Anthropocene" epoch, biologists have identified as a sixth mass extinction, and climatologists are warning is the greatest threat humanity has ever faced.

For the first time ever, our entire planet is endangered because of forces human beings have unleashed, and many of us have already begun to experience the consequences of this in our own lives. More frequent and devastating natural disasters, the Great Recession, and the coronavirus pandemic, widening inequality and rising authoritarianism, and increasing levels of mental illness are just a few of the many manifestations of this rapidly unfolding environmental, social, and economic polycrisis. As bad as the past couple of decades have been, they have likely only served a dress rehearsal for what is yet to come.

Unless we start making big changes now, things will get worse, but our politicians are tragically failing us and corporations have been allowed to continue their relentless pursuit of profit mostly unabated. Even the heroic efforts of professional activists and grassroots movements haven't been nearly enough. In this context, it's entirely understandable that many people who care about the state of our world and genuinely want to help bring forth a more just and regenerative future feel hopeless, overwhelmed, and confused about how and where to start. We all find ourselves caught between a way of life we know is rapidly coming to an end and a future that hasn't fully taken shape yet.

However, it's precisely this moment, when old systems and certainties are starting to break apart at record rates, that unprecedented opportunities for cultural and systemic transformation present themselves. When everything's going reasonably well, it's easier to simply float along with the mainstream, but we can no longer afford that luxury. Now is the time for all people of good conscience to lean into this challenge, step in off the sidelines, and begin to steer our own course.

The good news is we can start wherever we are and pick up whatever we need along the way. Because so many different things need to be done, everyone has an important role to play. We might choose to plant forests or grow food, serve as teachers or healers, run for office or block the path of a pipeline. What the specific thing is doesn't matter much. What matters most is that we all do something.

If enough of us lean in and take action, I believe we still have a chance to bend the long arc of history towards justice.[2] We don't lack any knowledge or resources necessary. The only thing that's been missing is our collective will.

Of course, actually bringing about a Great Transition[3] won't be easy, and there's no guarantee we'll succeed. However, the journey itself is its own reward. It offers us a chance to discover our deepest purpose, claim our power as agents of regeneration, and build community with others who are trying to do the same.

After all, isn't this what we've always wanted? To be thrust into being a hero in an epic saga? To tap into an inexhaustible source of inspiration and dedicate ourselves to a noble pursuit? Are we really satisfied with lives of quiet desperation, busying ourselves with hollow entertainment, unfulfilling jobs, and superficial relationships? Don't we feel called to greater adventure?

Evolutionary Change

These two words came to me more than a decade ago as a way to refer to an approach to life and activism that is uncommon but not unknown. Despite many attempts over the intervening years, I still haven't found a more succinct way to express this. From my perspective, the change we need to see in our world at this time is evolutionary in at least three ways.

1. **We've arrived at an evolutionary "bifurcation point" as a species:** The ecological destruction modern civilization has spread to nearly every part of our planet is patently unsustainable. If everyone alive today consumed like the average American, we would need 5.1 Earths to support us,[4] and global warming is now expected to cross the 1.5°C threshold within the next five years,[5] potentially triggering dangerous tipping points. Clearly, we can't continue this way much longer. Whether we have 5 years or 50 years, we need to start making big changes now. Humanity has come to an existential fork in the road where we must either evolve or suffer the consequences.

2. **The level of change currently needed can be thought of as an "evolutionary leap":** The status quo is no longer an option, and piecemeal reforms won't cut it. We need change on the scale of our fishy ancestors crawling up onto land for the first time or plants developing photosynthesis to harvest the energy of the sun. We need to find a new way to live in harmony with the Earth that works for at least eight billion people. This will require a massive overhaul of all of the systems we currently depend on as well as a reassessment of some of our most closely held values and beliefs. Ultimately, we'll need to become different people, not just consume different stuff.

3. **The approach I believe will be most effective is evolutionary in nature:** While we might dream of a sudden mass awakening or abrupt revolution that will instantly solve all our problems and set everything right, neither is likely to happen. Although it's crucial that we make change as quickly as possible, if we try to force it without creating the necessary conditions first, we won't succeed and will probably end up provoking counterproductive backlash. By working with reality as it is rather than how we want it to be, we might actually progress faster.

Rather than attempting to overpower natural processes, we would be wise to learn from them. Nature has much to teach us: not only the external nature of plants, animals, and ecosystems but also the internal nature of our most authentic being. Humans are not, as is commonly thought, a species apart. We are nature, human nature. We lean towards the light. We're blown by the wind. We're subject to the same laws of gravity, electromagnetism, and karma as everything else.

How a seed grows into a tree or a child develops into an adult stands in stark contrast to mechanistic conceptions of how life works. Evolutionary change is an organic process, more like a journey into the unknown than a formula we can rigidly follow. Over millennia, it's been called by many different names in many different languages by priests and poets, scientists and evolutionaries. All point towards a common underlying reality: a perennial philosophy of change.

For nearly two and a half decades now, I've been a dedicated student of how change occurs, testing out many different theories in my own life and work. Based on these experiences, I can confidently say that evolutionary change isn't just a nice idea. It's an entirely different way of being in the world that has the power to change everything.

In these increasingly chaotic times, change is inevitable but evolution is not. We can choose to lean in and be transformed by it or sit around and wait for it to show up on our doorstep. If we decide to lean in, why not learn how to turn it to our advantage? If not us, who? If not now, when?

Reclaiming Leadership

To bring about evolutionary change and planetary regeneration, I believe we need to reclaim the concept of leadership. While the leadership most people are familiar with tends to be individualistic and oppressive, there are other ways to engage in this essential practice that seek to support and empower rather than control and exploit. Instead of leadership being imposed by a few people perched atop a hierarchical pyramid, it can naturally bubble up from below and be broadly shared.

Fundamentally, leadership is power, which isn't inherently good or bad. It could be defined simply as our ability to influence our world. Power that's coercive is commonly referred to as "power over," while power that's shared is known as "power with." There's also "positional power," which is conferred by society, and "power within," which is innate. This book is all about developing our power within to expand our power with.

The time of the lone ranger-type hero is over. The challenges we face are far too big and urgent for any of us to hope to tackle them alone. Although somebody has to make the first move, individual leaders can be prone to egotism, myopia, and burnout. We need to cultivate diverse and resilient leaderful groups and movements to effectively unleash their collective genius.

Even in groups that claim to be leaderless, power dynamics are always present beneath the surface. If we choose to ignore them, they don't go away. We merely deprive ourselves of the opportunity to consciously shape them in accordance with our values.

However, if we can step into leadership in small ways to begin with and learn how to work with others to change things for the better, our leadership can eventually ripple out to positively influence the groups we are part of, the communities where we live, and the larger systems that we are enmeshed in. By stepping into our power, one person has the potential to inspire countless others over the course of a lifetime, and each of them has the potential to do the same.

This is the power of grassroots regenerative leadership and the reason I believe it may be the most powerful leverage point we have to bring about a Great Transition. In place of the ruinous exponential growth that has underpinned modern civilization thus far, we could unleash a tidal wave of compassion, cooperation, and creativity.

Although this might seem far-fetched, it might also be the best chance we've got. Our political leaders are constrained by public opinion, deadlocked in conflict, or worse; corporate leaders are obligated to maximize shareholder profits above all else; and nonprofit leaders are chronically underfunded and overmatched. I believe it's up to ordinary people like you and me to tip the balance of power. If we can do that, everything else will follow.

I'm not going to lie: this kind of leadership isn't something we can just do in our spare time, after work and on the weekends, whenever we feel like it. We have to learn to embody it in every aspect of our lives. We need to be willing to let go, over and over again, of who we thought we were to grow into the people we know we're capable of becoming. This process can be painful, lonely, and confusing at times. It's also, in my experience, undoubtedly worth it.

Who This Book Is For

The Regeneration Handbook has a lot to offer anyone who longs for a better world and wants to help make it a reality. Maybe you're feeling stuck in your life and are looking for a new perspective to shake things up, or maybe you want to get involved in making a meaningful difference but don't know how or where to start. Maybe you're already a committed activist, constantly searching out new insights. All of these are excellent reasons to read on.

Even if you don't know why you picked up this book, you might consider trusting your intuition. Sometimes, a lifelong journey unfolds from just the tiniest seed. This might be a glimpse of a vision, a spark of inspiration, or a moment of curiosity that eventually blossoms into something much greater.

We all need guides on our path to point out potential pitfalls and speed us on our way, but we also need companions who can share this journey and strengthen our determination to never give up. As author of this book, I see my role partly as a guide but mostly as a companion, reminding you of what you already know and encouraging you to trust that.

As you will see, *The Regeneration Handbook* draws heavily on my involvement with the international Transition Towns Movement over the past 15 years. For this reason, those who consider themselves Transitioners will find this book to be of particular interest. However, even if you've never heard of Transition, there's still much to be learned from this movement. I believe it's one of the most effective and inspiring movements in our world today, and many of its principles, strategies, and solutions can be adapted and applied to any effort for environmental, economic, or social regeneration.

Although my background as a founder of a local Transition Initiative, coordinator for a statewide hub, executive director of a national hub, and international Transition Trainer makes me somewhat uniquely qualified to write about this movement, I want to be clear from the outset that my views do not necessarily reflect those of all Transitioners. Part of the beauty and brilliance of the Transition Movement has always been its insistence that there's no one right way to do Transition.

Rather than seeking to make a definitive statement about what Transition is or isn't, my hope is that *The Regeneration Handbook* sparks discussion and inspires others to share their thoughts, especially those whose voices haven't been part of this conversation so far. Because I'm inherently limited by my perspective as a university-educated, middle-aged, straight, white male who has lived most of his life in urban and suburban areas throughout the US, I would very much like to hear more from BIPOC Transition leaders, those who live in other countries and rural areas, women, LGBTQ+ folks, and youth. I believe we're still only in the early stages of figuring out how the Transition process actually works, and nobody has all the answers. Only by sharing our experiences and insights with each other will we develop the collective wisdom needed to fundamentally transform our world.

What You'll Learn

While *The Regeneration Handbook* is rooted in my ongoing involvement with the Transition Movement, it draws from many other sources as well. It's been inspired and informed by the work of dozens of leading regenerative thinkers and doers spanning many different fields, including ecology and cosmology, psychology and sociology, organizational development and systems thinking, and activism and the arts. It also draws on my experiences as an anti-war and social justice activist, a wilderness instructor for at-risk and adjudicated youth, a devoted student and practitioner of Tibetan Buddhism, an organic farmer and Permaculture gardener, and someone who has lived in several different intentional communities.

You can think of this book as a kind of field guide for the evolutionary journey, surveying its inner, interpersonal, and collective dimensions while providing an abundance of tools, practices, and advice for every stage along the path. For this reason, I suggest reading it straight through at least once.

- **Chapter 2: Patterns of Evolution:** In the following chapter, I'll introduce you to four "meta-patterns" of Transformation, Expansion, Wholeness, and Balance. We'll examine their essential characteristics, how they appear in both nature and culture, and how they combine to form an integrated framework.

- **Chapter 3: My Evolutionary Journey:** Here, I offer my personal story as just one example of how evolutionary change can unfold over the course of a lifetime. Although my circumstances are far from universal, I believe my journey effectively demonstrates its power, its naturalness and humanity, and many of its key principles in action.

- **Chapters 4 and 5: Introducing Transition:** These two chapters shift focus from the individual to the collective, using the Transition Movement as a case study and model for evolutionary change in society. In "The Transition Story," we'll explore how this movement rapidly spread from its humble beginnings in 2005 and 2006 to more than 1,000 communities in over 50 countries worldwide. Then, in "The Five Stages of Transition," I'll expand on a theory of change from Transition Movement founder Rob

Hopkins' *Transition Companion* to show how local efforts can be scaled up and networked to bring about a tipping point for global regeneration.

- **Chapters 6 to 12: The Seven Essential Ingredients:** Each of these chapters focuses on one of the Seven Essential Ingredients of the Transition approach. Chapters on "Our Global Context" and "The Power of Vision" explore its philosophical underpinnings, while those on the "Inner Transition" and "Healthy Groups" address its individual and interpersonal dimensions. "Community Engagement" and "Practical Projects" detail the external activities of Transition Initiatives, while "Part of a Movement" reflects on how we might gain influence at national and international levels.

- **Chapter 13: Conclusion:** In this final chapter, I share some closing thoughts about why all of this really matters and how the forces of evolutionary change and regeneration might actually win out in the long run. I also offer suggestions for potential next steps and lead you through a personal action planning process.

While I've done my best to avoid speculation and only recommend what I've confirmed through my own experience, it's important to recognize the advice I offer may not be appropriate for you. Due to our different backgrounds, locations, preferences, and abilities, what's worked well for me might not for you. For this reason, I encourage you to question everything, reflect on your own experience, and judge for yourself what is and isn't likely to be helpful. Then, experiment with only that which seems most promising to you and see what happens.

The process of evolutionary change is truly never-ending. What may prove useful at one stage of your journey may not be at another. We always need to be iterating and fine-tuning our approach, repeatedly letting go of what's no longer working to create space for new strategies to take shape.

Eventually, we all need to become our own teachers, to travel out beyond the edges of all the maps that have been handed to us. From this perspective, this book can also be thought of as merely a jumping-off point for your own explorations. What you get out of it is ultimately up to you.

Patterns of Evolution

*In an ordinary English sentence, each word has one meaning, and
the sentence too has one simple meaning. In a poem, the meaning
is far more dense. Each word carries several meanings, and the
sentence as a whole carries an enormous density of interlocking
meanings, which together illuminate the whole. The same is
true for pattern languages. It is possible to make buildings by
stringing together patterns, in a rather loose way. A building
made like this is an assembly of patterns. It is not dense. It is not
profound. But it is also possible to put patterns together in such
a way that many many patterns overlap in the same physical
space: the building is very dense; it has many meanings captured
in a small space; and through this density, it becomes profound.*

— Christopher Alexander, et al., *A Pattern Language*[1]

Of all the courses I took as a graduate student in Environmental Leadership at Naropa University, my favorite was Transforming Systems. I was and continue to be fascinated by how living systems come together, break apart, reorganize, thrive, adapt, and evolve. Learning about esoteric concepts like autopoiesis, dissipative structures, and emergent properties still feels a bit like being initiated into the secret inner workings of the universe.[2]

To counteract the tendency of his students to become overly intoxicated by these ideas, our professor, Mark Wilding, wisely reminded us towards the beginning of almost every class that "The map is not the territory." By this, he meant that no concept, no matter how profound, can ever substitute for direct experience. Mark also frequently shared a corollary to this first axiom: "All models are wrong, but some are useful."

Whenever a map or model proves beneficial across many different contexts, we might reasonably call it a "pattern." This is the sense in which Christopher Alexander and his colleagues used this term in their 1977 book, *A Pattern Language: Towns, Buildings, Construction*. Over the course of 1,200 pages, they present 253 patterns related to the design of built environments, from organizing entire regions around the idea of "City Country Fingers" to the benefits of having a variety of "Different Chairs" in every room of a house. Taken all together and combined in various ways, these form what they called a "pattern language."

While *The Regeneration Handbook* is much shorter and structured quite differently from Alexander and company's massive tome, it can also be thought of as a kind of pattern language. Indeed, you'll find numerous patterns scattered throughout its pages.

The purpose of this chapter is to introduce you to four "meta-patterns" of Transformation, Expansion, Wholeness, and Balance. My hope is that, by providing some basic grounding in them here, you'll be able to identify other examples as they appear throughout the book.

Ultimately, our greatest power to affect change comes from weaving these four meta-patterns together. Because their logic often runs counter to conventional thinking, it's natural to question them at first. However, I hope you will eventually come to experience them as I have: as part of a single dynamic process that pervades our universe, fractally, at all levels.

Patterns of Transformation

Patterns of Transformation are the beating heart of evolutionary change. We can see this meta-pattern at work in nature in the turning of the seasons as well as in cycles of life, death, and rebirth. While modern society tends to ignore and deny the inevitability of death in favor of fantasizing about immortality and eternal youth, this clearly isn't how life works.

It's a harsh truth, but we can't be reborn without first going through a process of dying to our former selves, which can be extremely painful and disorienting. Nevertheless, this is the way life regenerates itself. Last season's crops need to be composted in the fall for the soil to burst forth in even greater abundance next spring. The caterpillar has to melt down into an unrecognizable goo before its "imaginal cells" can begin to resurrect it as a butterfly.

Because this dying process can be terrifying, it's important to remember that greater life always awaits us on the other side. In many traditional cultures, elders were available to guide young people through this treacherous passage. However, in our modern world, authentic elders can be difficult to find. Because most have not gone through the process of Transformation themselves, they're simply unable to help us.

While one might reasonably assume that Transformation looks like a line constantly angling upward or a circle that ends where it began, I've come to believe it's more accurately depicted as a U shape. Unlike a line, Transformation isn't straightforward, and unlike a circle, we don't end up in exactly the same place where we started. Instead, we are fundamentally changed in the process.

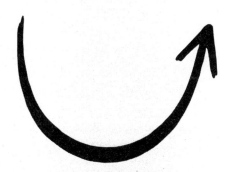

Figure 2.1: The archetypal U shape of Transformation.

This idea of Transformation as a U shape comes from Theory U, which was originally articulated by Peter Senge, Otto Scharmer, Joseph Jaworski, and Betty Sue Flowers in their 2005 book *Presence: An Exploration of Profound Change in People, Organizations, and Society.*[3] Their introduction explains how this pattern emerged from a series of interviews Scharmer and Jaworski conducted with more than 150 leading scientists and entrepreneurs about the nature of innovation. In one of these conversations, Brian Arthur, a prominent economist and Taoist practitioner, described his creative process as consisting of three distinct phases: "Observe, observe, observe," "Retreat and reflect," and "Act swiftly, with a natural flow."

Figure 2.2: Brian Arthur's three-stage model.

In the years following the publication of *Presence*, Scharmer mapped out this basic model in greater detail, culminating in the release of *Theory U: Leading from the Future as It Emerges* in 2009.[4] During that time, he also became a senior lecturer at the Sloan School of Management at MIT and founded the Presencing Institute, which is described as "an action research platform at the intersection of science, consciousness, and profound social and organizational change."

As it's currently understood, Theory U consists of seven distinct stages. By suspending our habitual reactions, we can stop mindlessly repeating the patterns of the past (Downloading), and begin Seeing and Sensing in a more direct and unfiltered way. This eventually produces an internal shift (Presencing) that enables us to move into progressively more effective action through Crystallizing, Prototyping, and Performing.

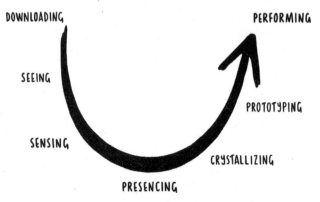

Figure 2.3: The seven stages of Theory U.

Although I find Theory U to be a particularly useful map of Transformation, there are many other models that are strikingly similar. One is the Hero's Journey, described by Joseph Campbell in his classic text, *The Hero with a Thousand Faces*.[5] Comparing mythologies from a wide range of Indigenous cultures and religious traditions around the world, he uncovered a common pattern: a Departure from everyday reality, followed by a perilous Initiation in the depths, followed by the hero's Return to the ordinary world, bearing new insights and gifts.

Figure 2.4: The Hero's Journey, plotted against a U shape.

Because so many different patterns of Transformation align so closely with each other, it's reasonable to conclude that they're all pointing towards the same universal truth. Throughout this book, you'll encounter this meta-pattern applied to inner Transformation in the Spiral of the Work That Reconnects, interpersonal Transformation in the Stages of Group Development, and collective Transformation in the Five Stages of Transition:

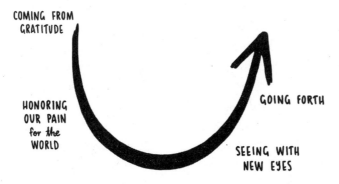

Figure 2.5: The Spiral of the Work That Reconnects, plotted against a U shape.

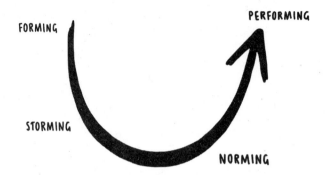

Figure 2.6: The Stages of Group Development, plotted against a U shape.

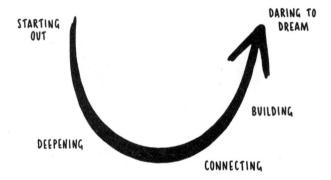

Figure 2.7: The Five Stages of Transition, plotted against a U shape.

Whatever language is used to describe Transformation, the following general principles underlie the process itself:

- **Transformation unfolds in predictable stages:** Some models are divided into dozens while others have as few as two, but their basic outline is the same: we need to let go of who we think we are and what we think we know to make space for something new to emerge. It's a process of moving downward and inward from (our head to our heart), then expanding upward and outward (from our heart to our hands).

- **We can't skip stages:** As much as we might want to jump directly from point A (our current reality) to point B (a desired future), this typically isn't possible. We usually have to embark on a circuitous journey to reach our destination. The quickest route between two points is often not the most direct. If we are climbing a mountain, we'll likely need to take switchbacks to reach the top. Although we do need to leap sometimes, trying to make a long journey by leaping from one spot to the next is insanity. We'll tire ourselves out long before we get there.

- **Transformation is challenging, but it's ultimately worth it:** Whenever we leave behind familiar territory to venture into the unknown, we inevitably encounter many difficulties. Nevertheless, if we persist on our path, we cannot help learning a great many things along the way and growing tremendously as people.

It's important to note that this journey through the U can manifest in various ways. It can happen in the blink of an eye or unfold gradually throughout a lifetime. We may be involved in several U processes simultaneously and find ourselves at different stages in relation to each. Once you know what to look for, you'll start seeing this meta-pattern everywhere.

Patterns of Expansion

While patterns of Transformation can be used to describe a complete process, they can also be thought of as just one step in a much greater journey. If we look at a spiral, we can see that it's actually made up of a series of U shapes. This is an image of the union of the meta-patterns of Transformation and Expansion.

Figure 2.8: The union of Transformation and Expansion.

A spiral is not just a series of U shapes, however. It has an element of Expansion in it as well. If we look at a spiral from its top or bottom, the essence of Expansion is revealed. It appears as a series of concentric circles, like ripples from a stone thrown into the middle of a pond:

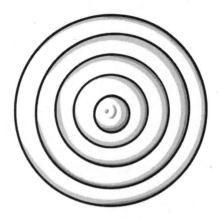

Figure 2.9: The archetypal ripple pattern of Expansion.

Patterns of Expansion are found everywhere in nature. Human beings always start off as babies, infants, children, and adolescents before maturing into adults. In a similar way, an oak always goes through the process of being a seed and a sapling before it becomes a tree. It never happens that a tree just spontaneously erupts, fully formed, from a seed.

If properly nurtured, trees and people and all other forms of life gradually evolve in the direction of their highest potential. Atoms join to make molecules, which combine to form organelles, cells, tissues, organs, organisms, and ecosystems. Each stage in the development of life introduces new circumstances and conditions, new challenges and opportunities.

An especially vivid example of this meta-pattern is the process of ecological succession. Consider this poetic passage from Toby Hemenway's *Gaia's Garden: A Guide to Home-Scale Permaculture*:

When plants first colonize bare earth—for example, an abandoned farm—a progression begins. Certain types of annual grasses, herbs, and flowers are the first flora to arrive, and because of their penchant for speedy colonization, they are called pioneer plants. They're well adapted to invading naked or disturbed soil and mantling the floral emptiness with green. Pioneer plants fill the vegetal vacuum and restart the cycles of life. We know most of this fast-colonizing horde as weeds: crabgrass, dandelion, sheep sorrel, pigweed, plantain, chicory, wild lettuce, and many more. Abandoned fields and fresh earth are their milieu, and they have a job to do: sheltering the bare soil from erosive rains, and ferrying nutrients from deep in the soil to the surface where they can be used. These fast-growing, short-lived pioneers preserve and restore the fertility of disturbed ground.

If these weeds are left alone, in a few seasons the short, early annuals are crowded and shaded out by a taller, mostly perennial crew. In the northern half of the United States, these include asters, fireweed, goldenrod, spurge, perennial grasses, and many others. The dense foliage, branching stems, and many textures of the tall weeds offer more niches for insects and birds to shelter, breed, and feed. The amount of living matter, called biomass, increases as nutrients and sunlight are gathered and transformed into tough stalks, thick greenery, and hardy seeds, which in turn become food for insects and other animals. In this way, life quickly gets a firm toehold on the bare ground. Where before the elements needed for life were confined to a thin band of topsoil, now these nutrients surge in a much thicker layer of vegetation filled with mobile animals. Life is scaffolding its way into new territory.

The progression from bare earth to short annual weeds to tall perennials is called *succession*. If allowed to continue, in five to fifteen years the weedy field will be clothed instead with perennial shrubs. With enough rain and fertility, in two or more decades, the shrubs will give way to a young forest.[6]

Life naturally creates the conditions for more and more life to thrive over time. It's only when we're out of alignment with nature's patterns and try to impose our will on them that we experience persistent degradation. Of course, accidents and disasters happen, but they're only temporary. Like periodic wildfires that reinvigorate the health of forests, they can even be beneficial.

Another pattern of Expansion worth noting here comes from the practice of Permaculture design. In laying out a homestead, one typically starts with one's home (Zone 0) and the space immediately surrounding it (Zone 1) because that's where most people spend most of their time. Zone 1 is where Permaculturalists typically locate their annual vegetable and herb gardens because they need to be irrigated and tended to every day during the growing season. One might keep bees, livestock, and compost in Zone 2, at a distance where they can be checked on frequently but not so close that one has to worry about stings and bad smells. Zone 3 is usually where perennial crops, such as fruit trees, are grown. Zone 4 is often reserved for foraging, and Zone 5 is meant to be left entirely wild.

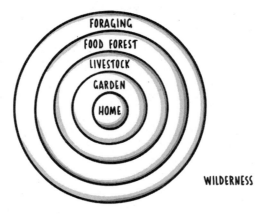

Figure 2.10: Permaculture Zones.

As with many of the other models I present throughout this book, this is a greatly simplified description of Permaculture Zones. They're almost never perfect circles. and what's contained within each zone differs, depending on the characteristics of the site and the aims of its developers. Nevertheless, Permaculture Zones effectively demonstrate a natural progression from what is closest to us (over which we have the most influence) to what is farthest away (over which we have the least control).

Translating this from the realm of Permaculture design to evolutionary change, Zone 0 can be thought of as our personal development work, the foundation upon which everything else rests. Zone 1 represents home and family life; Zone 2, our involvement in our wider community; Zone 3, any regional or national influence we might have; and Zone 4, whatever impact we're able to muster on a global scale. I tend to think of Zone 5 as the vast universe beyond Earth, which remains almost entirely beyond human interference and understanding.

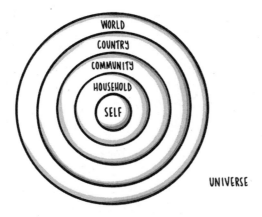

Figure 2.11: Zones of evolutionary change.

While we may desire influence at national and international levels, it's only by working with Zones 0, 1, and 2 first that we have any hope of making a positive contribution in Zones 3 and 4. This doesn't mean we need to perfect each zone before moving onto the next, but the more experience we have cultivating change in ourselves, at home, and in our local communities, the more likely it is that our efforts to bring about larger-scale transformation will succeed.

It's also important to recognize that we don't leave behind earlier zones as we progress. Even if we happen to find ourselves in positions of national or global leadership, it's essential that we continue to work on ourselves and stay in touch with the grassroots. Otherwise, we can easily become ungrounded, intoxicated by our own sense of importance and disconnected from reality.

Patterns of Wholeness

In addition to the meta-patterns of Transformation and Expansion, which represent the vertical dimension of evolutionary change, there are the meta-patterns of Wholeness and Balance, which constitute its horizontal axis. The main difference between these two is that "vertical" change refers to processes that only unfold over time, while "horizontal" change describes the development of innate capacities.[7]

In reality, these two dimensions aren't separate. Wholeness and Balance run like threads throughout our journey, evolving as we transition from stage to stage and level to level.

We observe patterns of Wholeness in nature when we look at how a limited number of elements combine to create a world of dazzling diversity or how various organs, parts, and systems cooperate to make a body dance. Often, we seek to avoid this level of complexity by boiling everything down to just one or two factors, but a monoculture with only one or two species cannot be sustained.

Wholeness, in the context of this book, is partly about becoming a more well-rounded person, developing all of our innate capacities so we can thrive in any situation. However, patterns of Wholeness can also be applied to groups, communities, and movements. Different circumstances call for different energies and approaches, and on the journey of evolutionary change, we need them all.

The archetypal form of Wholeness can be visualized as a mandala, a sacred circle with its essence firmly planted in the center, radiating outward to encompass a variety of manifestations. In Tibetan Buddhist iconography,

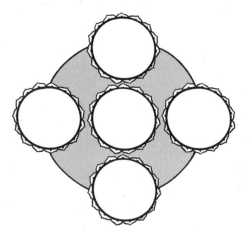

Figure 2.12: The archetypal mandala of Wholeness.

mandalas are sometimes visualized as royal palaces with a central deity surrounded by four gates. In some North American Indigenous cultures, these four gates are depicted as the four directions of a medicine wheel.

The Five Buddha families are a particularly potent example of this meta-pattern. In the center is the Buddha Buddha family, which represents enlightened spaciousness. It is surrounded in the East by the Vajra Buddha family, which represents enlightened clarity; in the South by the Ratna Buddha family, which represents enlightened richness; in the West by the Padma Buddha family, which represents enlightened passion; and in the North by the Karma Buddha family, which represents enlightened activity.[8]

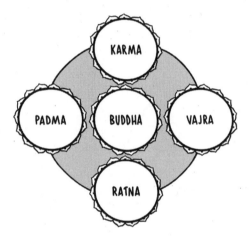

Figure 2.13: The Mandala of the Five Buddha families.

Although most people naturally gravitate towards some Buddha families more than others, the point is to cultivate all five kinds of wisdom. This is a different approach than is commonly taken in relation to astrology or popular personality tests like Myers-Briggs or the Enneagram. While these models help us identify our natural strengths and predispositions, they don't usually encourage us towards Wholeness. For example, if we're a Leo, we don't necessarily think about how we might become a better Taurus, Gemini, or Cancer.

Other patterns of Wholeness you'll come across in this book include the Four Quadrants of Ken Wilber, which integrate the inner with the outer and the individual with the collective; the Permaculture Flower, with its seven petals representing different aspects of society and pistil containing core Permaculture ethics and design principles; and the Transition Animal, with its four legs, eyes, heart, and surrounding environment representing the Seven Essential Ingredients of the Transition model:

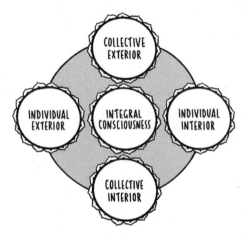

Figure 2.14: The Four Quadrants of Ken Wilber, arranged as a mandala.

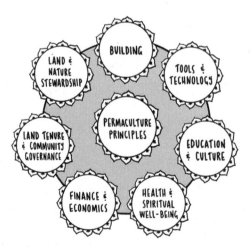

Figure 2.15: The Permaculture Flower, arranged as a mandala.

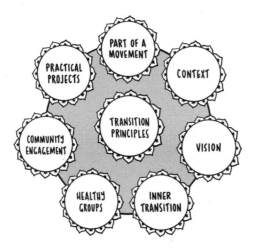

Figure 2.16: The Transition Animal, arranged as a mandala.

Patterns of Balance

Balance is often thought of as a static state, but not even death is truly static. Life, as living systems science tells us, exists in a dynamic state far from equilibrium. As such, Balance is constantly in flux, and there's no magic formula that can tell us how to find it. Instead, we have to experiment and engage our intuition to pinpoint the sweet spot.

There's a famous story in Buddhism about a sitar player who asked the historical Buddha how to work with his mind in meditation. The Buddha replied by turning the question around on the sitar player, asking him how he tuned his instrument. After reflecting for a moment, the sitar player replied: "Not too loose, not too tight." In other words, you know it when you hear it.

In nature, we see patterns of Balance at work in the alternation of day and night, predator-prey relationships, and negative (or self-balancing) feedback loops. A classic example of a self-balancing feedback loop is a thermostat. When the temperature in your house rises above a certain point, your thermostat senses that and temporarily shuts off your heat. Then, when the temperature falls back below that same point, your heat automatically kicks back on again.

Most of Earth's natural cycles, such as the carbon cycle, have evolved to function this way. Historically, plants, animals, oceans, and soil have all worked together to keep levels of carbon dioxide in our atmosphere relatively stable. However, since people began digging up and burning massive amounts of fossil fuels that took millions of years to form, we have upset that delicate balance, bringing about disastrous consequences in just a few short centuries.

Evolutionary change also harnesses the power of positive (or self-amplifying) feedback loops, but we need to be extremely careful with them. Although self-amplifying loops can be revolutionary, they can easily spiral out of control. An example of this is the effect of climate change on Earth's polar regions, where increased temperatures have caused ice to melt, exposing darker land and ocean beneath. These darker surfaces, in turn, absorb more heat, warming the planet further and melting more ice even faster.

The yin-yang, associated with Taoist philosophy, is perhaps the most well-known symbol of Balance. With its swirling patterns of dark and light, each containing a bit of the other, it represents interdependence and harmony among opposites:

Figure 2.17: The archetypal yin-yang of Balance.

Normally, we try to draw towards ourselves everything we think will benefit us while pushing away whatever appears unfamiliar, threatening, or unpleasant. While this approach to life has its logic, the problem is that we don't always know what will help and what will hurt us. If we only seek out that which is comfortable, pleasurable, and easy, avoiding anything that's difficult, we'll eventually find ourselves stunted, arrested in our development. I know many people who choose to focus only on the "positive" aspects of life, rejecting the widespread suffering of our world as too "negative" to even contemplate. If we do this, however, we'll end up naive, uncompassionate, and small. To realize our fullest potential, we need to embrace the totality of our experience, whatever that may be.

The meta-pattern of Balance can also be expressed as a spectrum or paradox: a seeming contradiction that isn't really a contradiction at all. Ultimately, we need to abandon all fixed ideas and dualistic thinking. While philosophers have debated fate versus free will for thousands of years, most have failed to realize that life isn't an either/or. It's a both/and. Rarely is the answer black or white, and there are many beautiful colors in between.

Patterns of Balance in this book include the inseparability of self and other, freedom and limitation, action and reflection, and challenge and opportunity. They are also evident in the ways that Wholeness and Balance, like Transformation and Expansion, complement each other. We can imagine the yin-yang of Balance being placed at the center of the mandala of Wholeness and radiating out from there. In seeking to cultivate Wholeness, we not only need to engage and develop every part but also ensure each part is continuously held in Balance.

Figure 2.18: The union of Wholeness and Balance.

Similarly, in attempting to envision the relationship between horizontal and vertical change, we should try to avoid imagining them as separate processes. Evolutionary change isn't a spiral placed on top of a mandala, like a vase on a table. It is more like a spiral pulsing with mandalas or a mandala twisting itself into a spiral. While this may be difficult to visualize, it points to the nondualistic nature of evolutionary change. It is an all-of-the-above, complexity-oriented approach.

My Evolutionary Journey

He not busy being born is busy dying.

— Bob Dylan, "It's Alright, Ma (I'm Only Bleeding)"[1]

At this point, I'd like to share my story with you, not only to give you a better sense of who I am as the author of this book, but more importantly, to demonstrate how the abstract theory of the previous chapter can actually manifest in our lived experience. Although my circumstances are far from universal, I trust that my story will convey just how human and natural, challenging and rewarding, practical and profound the evolutionary journey can be.

I find personal stories like this to be valuable because they communicate the beautiful messiness of three-dimensional existence in a way that two-dimensional maps and models simply can't. They help us feel the subtle textures of the path and see our own lives reflected in those of others.

When I first read Mahatma Gandhi's autobiography, *The Story of My Experiments with Truth*,[2] more than two decades ago, I remember being struck by the fact that he didn't set out to become a world-changing figure. Gandhi only became involved in activism after experiencing discrimination first-hand while practicing law in South Africa. Although he eventually became a larger-than-life legend, it's clear from his own words that he didn't have everything figured out from the beginning. He was basically making it up as he went along, just like the rest of us.

Looking back on my own (far more humble) journey, I can see that it was only by believing steadfastly in myself that I became the person I am today and only by remaining open to unexpected twists and turns in my path that I found my true calling. If I had settled for a more conventional and predictable existence, my life would have almost certainly been easier, but it wouldn't have been nearly as interesting. I'm far from perfect, but I'm always trying, always learning, always growing. I believe that's all we can ask from anyone. We are human, after all.

While an attentive reader will also notice the meta-patterns of Expansion, Wholeness, and Balance at work in my story, my journey has primarily been one of Transformation. For this reason, each of the following sections begins with a brief description of one of the seven stages of Theory U, followed by the corresponding part of my narrative.

Downloading

Moving towards a future possibility requires us to become aware of—and abandon—the dominant mode of downloading that causes us to continuously reproduce the patterns of the past.

— Otto Scharmer, *Theory U* [3]

Whether it's Frodo in the Shire or Buddha Shakyamuni in his palace, every great adventure story begins with its protagonist dwelling in a state of relative ignorance. While we may long for a more meaningful existence, we probably don't even know what that might look like yet. Because this is how we all start, we can't blame ourselves for Downloading.

Downloading is the act of indiscriminately applying patterns of thought and behavior that are rooted in past experience to present situations. This can manifest as simply doing what we've always done or sheepishly conforming to the expectations of others. Something comes up and we react automatically, in our own habitual way. Many of us are familiar with Downloading as "being on autopilot."

Although Downloading can be appropriate in situations when the task before us is familiar and straightforward, such as turning a doorknob or tying our shoelaces, it becomes a problem when we attempt to approach more complex and novel challenges this way. Especially in the face of unprecedented crisis, Downloading is woefully insufficient.

DOWNLOADING

Figure 3.1: The first stage of Theory U.

I was born in 1981 in Wellesley, Massachusetts, a wealthy suburb of Boston, as the only child of Donald and Nancy Hall. My father was a management consultant who traveled frequently for work, advising corporations in the US and abroad how to cut costs and run their businesses more efficiently. My mother stayed home to take care of me, volunteered for several local organizations, and dabbled in Republican politics.

We lived in an old Tudor house at the bottom of a hill on a quiet, tree-lined street. We celebrated birthdays and holidays together, and traveled frequently on vacation. My father would read mystery novels in his spare time, while my mother would cook dinner from scratch most nights. My parents seemed to actually love each other and rarely spoke a harsh word to me. Occasionally, my mother teased my father by calling him "plain vanilla," but it was all in good fun.

I learned to speak and read early, but was mostly unremarkable as a child. I got straight As in public school and attended church with my parents, played sports and video games, and tried to fit in with the cool kids. I was generally awkward and shy, but made it through my elementary and middle school years relatively unscathed.

Nevertheless, at some level, I always felt at odds with this seemingly idyllic manifestation of the American Dream. I felt most of the people around me were superficial and inauthentic, and to my adolescent mind, life appeared pointless and unreal. Without any way to make sense of these feelings, I internalized them. In my early teenage years, all I had was my angst.

As I grew older, I started to push back against this sleepy conformity in the only ways I knew how: by hanging out with the wrong crowd, sneaking out at night to meet girls, smoking, drinking, and experimenting with drugs. I know this worried my parents terribly, but I didn't care. I was doing whatever I could to assert my independence. I was a rebel without a clue.

Seeing

The shift from downloading to seeing is simple—
although not always painless.

— Otto Scharmer, *Theory U*[4]

It usually takes some kind of cataclysm to interrupt our Downloading and initiate Seeing. Of course, we can choose to cling to our ignorance, but if we're courageous enough to suspend our habitual patterns and keep our eyes and minds open, we'll inevitably notice a lot we hadn't before. Though much of what we see at first is likely to be deeply unsettling, we need to persist for the transformational process to take hold.

This is a far cry from our default mode of being, which operates on the principle of "Been there, done that." When we walk through our world like this, we don't really see or experience anything. Every flowering cherry tree fades into the background, and every bustling city becomes merely a stopover en route to somewhere else. Every person we meet is just a means to an end. In such a closed system, there are no possibilities for learning or growth.

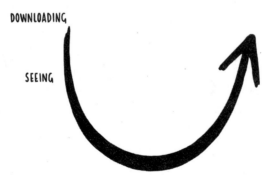

Figure 3.2: The second stage of Theory U.

After I graduated from middle school, my parents sent me away to a private boarding school that was only a 30-minute drive from where we lived. I know they wanted me to get the best education possible and probably hoped it would straighten me out, but my delinquency only deepened. Towards the end of my sophomore year, I was nearly expelled, and after moving with my parents to Sarasota, Florida, I was arrested for buying beer with fake ID.

Fortunately, something else happened around that same time that changed my life forever and set me on a completely different path. My then-girlfriend invited me to go on a 21-day multi-element Outward Bound course in Maryland with her. Although I had never camped out a day in my life before, I immediately signed up. I probably would have done anything for her.

The first part of the trip was miserable. We were sailing on the Chesapeake Bay, and it rained nonstop for days. The windbreaker I had foolishly brought instead of a rain jacket wasn't up to the task, and as a result, I was continuously soaked to the bone and freezing, huddled with about a dozen of my peers underneath a leaky tarp.

I don't remember much about the second week spent canoeing on the Potomac River, but the third week, backpacking in Savage National Forest, was highly memorable. I recall starting to feel at home in the woods, experiencing a ruggedness and self-confidence I hadn't previously known. I was also beginning to appreciate my instructors, one of whom was an African American ex-Marine with massive dreadlocks named Naya.

I had never met anyone like him before: smart, strong, creative, and kind. He composed spontaneous poetry and taught me tai chi on my wilderness solo. Naya took me and my girlfriend under his wing, and when we graduated, gifted us books on Eastern philosophy straight out of the trunk of his car. Although I would meet many others like him in the decades to come, he was the first to help me recognize who I really was. I knew instantly that I wanted to be like him.

While it's hard to say exactly how much was Naya's influence and how much was due to me deeply connecting with nature for the first time, when I returned home, I was a completely different person. I worked hard to repair my relationship with my parents, began to apply myself at school, and quit hanging out with old friends. I started meditating and writing poetry, and went from eating fast food to becoming a vegetarian practically overnight. The following year, I received an award for Most Improved Student and was accepted to New York University.

Sensing

When moving from seeing to sensing,
perception begins to happen from the whole field.

— Otto Scharmer, *Theory U*[5]

Where Seeing is about opening ourselves up to new experiences and information, Sensing is about feeling our way into what it all means. It's literally the act of making sense of our situation, not by imposing our concepts on it, but by using both our intellect and intuition to make new connections and develop greater clarity.

Our brains are able to process incredibly large amounts of information and weave them into complex webs of meaning. However, our thinking minds are really only able to work in a linear fashion, one dot at a time. They don't comprehend wholes. That's the job of the innate intelligence that resides in our bodies and hearts: to synthesize the dizzying array of inputs we receive and ultimately tell us what to do.

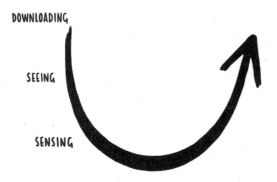

Figure 3.3: The third stage of Theory U.

When I arrived in New York City, just after the turn of the new millennium, everything felt like it was destined to go my way. I remember introducing myself to strangers on the subway and picking up trash in Washington Square Park between classes, both of which earned me many concerned looks from world-weary New Yorkers. I was continually on fire with inspiration, writing lots of poetry, dating an aspiring photographer, and hanging out at underground blues clubs on the weekends. My life was taking off like a rocket ship with no end in sight.

Then, less than a month later, my father died suddenly of a heart attack. I immediately flew back home and delivered the eulogy at his funeral. I'd planned to stay longer, but after a few weeks, my mother urged me to return to New York to continue my studies. I thought I was basically fine. It was only years later that I realized what a profound impact my father's death had on me.

In spite of my grief (and probably as a way to cope with it), I started exploring how I might make some positive contribution to society. Through my exposure to big-city life and progressive politics, I was beginning to understand just how much suffering existed in the world and how incredibly privileged I was. This impressed upon me a tremendous sense of responsibility to give back.

One day as I was walking to class, I found myself strangely attracted to a flier with a small Tibetan flag on it that was pinned to a bulletin board in the hallway. It was advertising an event with a former political prisoner who had escaped torture by the Chinese government. That night, I joined the NYU chapter of Students for a Free Tibet and ended up helping to run it for three years. We hosted Buddhist monks and other Tibetan dignitaries for speeches and cultural performances, collected thousands of signatures to free political prisoners, and organized demonstrations at the Chinese Consulate.

Then, when 9/11 happened, I joined the anti-war movement, protesting in Times Square just as the US was beginning to bomb Afghanistan, and marching with over a million people in London during the run-up to the invasion of Iraq. This led me to what used to be called the "anti-globalization" movement, as well as many others.

Once I graduated from college, I had to get a job. Not knowing what I wanted to do, I reflected on my experience with Outward Bound five years earlier and wondered if I might be able to work for them. After discovering they had a program in Florida, Georgia, and South Carolina for at-risk and adjudicated youth, I applied and was accepted. For the next two years, my co-instructors and I guided students on 20-to-30-day flatwater canoeing expeditions. We taught them how to camp, tie knots, and paddle a canoe, as well as how to work with their emotions, respond to conflicts nonviolently, and make better life decisions.

While I loved spending so much time in nature and giving back in this way, I eventually burned out like so many others before me. After leaving Outward Bound and returning to Sarasota in 2006, I worked at an outdoors store for a few months before a friend told me about a local organic farm that might be looking for help. Working hard in the fields day after day at Jessica's Organic Farm healed me, and I grew to appreciate the simple goodness of farmwork. Nevertheless, something in me remained unsettled, still searching for where I truly belonged.

Having come to believe that climate change would be the defining issue of the twenty-first century, I started volunteering with the Sarasota Network for Climate Action. I sensed this was what I wanted to do with my life, but recognized I could only accomplish so much after work and on the weekends. While I longed to devote myself full-time to climate activism, there were few if any such jobs available in Sarasota in 2007. As a result, I was again left wondering what to do.

Presencing

The key difference is that sensing shifts the place of perception to the current whole while presencing shifts the place of perception to the source of an emerging future whole— to a future possibility that is seeking to emerge.

— Otto Scharmer, *Theory U* [6]

As we see and sense more and more deeply, we are naturally drawn into a state of Presencing at the bottom of the U. At this pivotal stage, we are encouraged to retreat and reflect on questions like "Who is my Self?" and

"What is my Work?" Although sustained introspection inevitably produces an upwelling of insight, this usually doesn't happen right away. Typically, we have to wrestle with the angel of our not-knowing for a long while first.

Most people avoid Presencing because they correctly intuit that if they open themselves up to their deepest truth, what emerges may be unlike anything they expected. We might have to quit our comfortable job or finally end a codependent relationship. Once we've received an essential message from the depths, however, we can't go back and pretend we didn't hear it. That way lies madness.

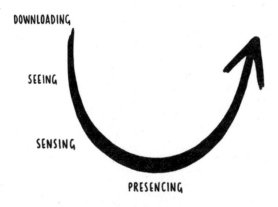

Figure 3.4: The fourth stage of Theory U.

Not knowing how to proceed, I sat down to envision my future. As I reflected on what I truly wanted and wrote down the answers that came to me in my journal, I gradually realized what I'd been looking for: a creative approach to environmental activism that was aligned with spiritual principles. The political activism I had been previously exposed to clearly wasn't it. With its problem-based orientation, us-versus-them mentality, and single-issue focus, it wasn't addressing root causes or offering holistic alternatives. Furthermore, a lot of the activists I'd met tended not to be very well-informed and seemed to be driven by a heady mix of guilt, fear, and self-righteousness. I longed to find a different way, one I could believe in with my whole mind and heart.

When I was at NYU, I had dreamed of dropping out to attend the Jack Kerouac School of Disembodied Poetics at Naropa University, but didn't have the courage to do that at the time. So when I learned Naropa had a master's program in Environmental Leadership, I jumped at the opportunity to apply. Although, practically speaking, a master's degree from Naropa wouldn't mean much, I had the sense it was exactly what I needed to move forward.

Shortly after being accepted, I packed all my belongings and drove out to Boulder, Colorado, knowing I was taking a leap of faith. Fortunately, the program turned out to be an amazing fit for my interests. I took classes in Transforming Systems, the New Science and Its Cultural Applications, Inner Work for Environmental Leaders, Groups as Living Systems, Authentic Leadership, and more in a close cohort of 16 students. We participated in workshops with Joanna Macy on the Work That Reconnects and Marshall Rosenberg on Nonviolent Communication, and even spent a week together in deep retreat in the Rockies.

While some of my fellow students were disappointed because they expected a more academically rigorous program that would easily translate into a job, I knew I wasn't looking for a conventional career. Naropa wasn't just about showing up and plugging into a formula. It was about engaging one's whole being in a process of transformation. As such, it gave me the perspective and confidence I needed to lead and helped set me on my path.

Crystallizing

If this connection is established, the first thing that happens is: nothing. It's just a connection. But, when we succeed in keeping that connection to our deeper source of knowing alive, we begin to better tune into emerging future possibilities.

— Otto Scharmer, *Theory U* [7]

What emerges in Presencing is still relatively shapeless, but Crystallizing begins to fill in the details and bring our vision to life. I often visualize this stage as holding a diamond in the palm of my hand, turning it over and over again to really get to know it from every angle. Through this kind of contemplation, we breathe life into our original spark of inspiration until it becomes a fire.

Although our vision doesn't need to be crystal clear before we move into Prototyping, if we rush the process and act prematurely, we usually regret it. Time spent Crystallizing isn't wasted. It's an essential part of our overall journey.

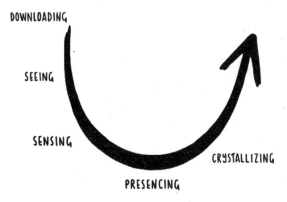

Figure 3.5: The fifth stage of Theory U.

The Naropa program had one other key component I haven't mentioned yet: an Applied Leadership Project. Instead of writing a thesis that few people would ever read, we were required to find a local organization to partner with and collaboratively design a project that would make a real difference.

By the time I needed to make a decision about who to partner with, I had already attended a few events organized by Boulder County Going Local, which was one of the stars of Post Carbon Institute's Relocalization Network.[8] In all of my searching, I'd never encountered anything like it before. I was impressed by its leaders' sophisticated understanding of complex global issues, intrigued by their vision of a more conscious and cooperative future, and inspired by their practical, bottom-up approach to change-making. It was a revelation for me to realize that we don't have to wait for anyone to give us permission to begin creating the world we want. For the first time, I felt like I had found something I could put my whole heart and soul into.

The first and second times I reached out to Boulder County Going Local's co-founders, Michael Brownlee and Lynette Marie Hanthorn, I received no response, but the third time proved the charm. We met and hit it off immediately. Having recently returned from Totnes, England, the birth-place of the Transition Movement, Michael and Lynette Marie had decided to apply for recognition as the first official Transition Initiative in North America. One of my first tasks as an intern was to fill out that application.

After my internship. I was hired on part-time, then full-time once I graduated. We became Transition Boulder County, then Transition Colorado, helping to launch a dozen Transition Initiatives throughout the state. My title was Education & Outreach Coordinator. I organized our Great Reskilling program and served as the primary point of contact for local leaders statewide.

During this time, I was also introduced to the closely related movements of Permaculture and intentional communities. In 2007, following a friend's recommendation, I applied to live at the Chrysalis Cooperative in downtown Boulder. While I had only the vaguest idea of what an intentional community was before moving in, I loved it so much that I've lived in co-ops whenever I've had the chance ever since. The following year, I completed a 72-hour Permaculture Design Course at the Central Rocky Mountain Permaculture Institute and have now grown a garden every year for the past decade and a half.

I'd long been fascinated by the topic of leadership, and my studies at Naropa pushed me even further in that direction. I saw supporting grass-roots leaders as a real need and a way to multiply my impact. Combining what I'd learned at Naropa with everything I was learning from the Transition Movement, I designed a 16-week course in Deepening Community Leadership as my Applied Leadership Project and taught it through Transition Colorado in 2009.

However, a realization began to dawn on me that if I really wanted to help local leaders succeed and thrive, even the best theory wasn't going to be enough. I needed to experience for myself the nitty-gritty of starting and developing a local Transition Initiative from scratch. I had learned so much from my mentors, but also had a lot of my own ideas that I wanted to test out in the world.

Prototyping

Having established a connection to source (presencing) and having clarified a sense of the future that wants to emerge (crystallizing), the next stage in the U process is to explore the future by doing (prototyping).

— Otto Scharmer, *Theory U* [9]

The spirit of Prototyping is that of an experiment. Because we've thoroughly seen, sensed, presenced, and crystallized, we can now be confident that we've prepared ourselves the best we can for actually launching our idea into the world.

As exciting as this is, Prototyping can also be terrifying because we finally have to share our beautiful dream with others and possibly fall flat on our face. This can manifest as analysis paralysis, letting the perfect be the enemy of ever getting started. However, if we can summon the courage needed to step forward, remain open to feedback, and modify our approach as we go, both our failures and successes can serve as stepping stones, leading us onward from where we are now to who we might become.

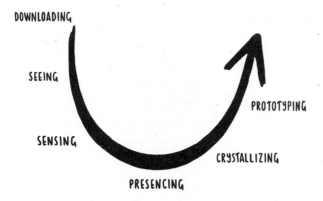

Figure 3.6: The sixth stage of Theory U.

Once I decided to leave Transition Colorado, my first thought was to reach out to the former leaders of Transition Boulder, which had recently disbanded, to find out if there was any interest in trying to revive it. However, these conversations were almost universally discouraging. Nearly everyone said they felt there were already too many groups working on similar issues locally.

I was still wondering what to do when I returned to Sarasota to visit my mother over the Christmas holiday. While I was there, a friend offered to organize a potluck for others to hear me speak about Transition. Although my presentation that night was informal and brief, those who showed up responded with a freshness and enthusiasm I'd previously found lacking in ultra-progressive Boulder.

Sarasota was and continues to be politically conservative. Nevertheless, at that time, a lot of changes were starting to happen that I took to be encouraging signs. In the few short years since I'd left, a local nonprofit radio station had gone on the air, a co-working community for young entrepreneurs had been established, and new farmers' markets and community gardens were popping up everywhere. I felt Transition could play a valuable role in this emerging ecosystem, filling an important niche and helping to weave related groups into a powerful movement.

So, in the spring of 2010, with just a vision of what could be and a few thousand dollars in my bank account, I moved back home to Florida to start Transition Sarasota. In the beginning, I modeled it after Transition Colorado, founding it as a fairly conventional nonprofit organization with myself as executive director and focusing our efforts on growing our local food system. Over the next six and a half years, we organized hundreds of educational events, cultivated a diverse array of partnerships, ran several highly successful programs, and attracted significant media attention. By the fall of 2016, we were poised for yet another great leap forward, but I finally ran out of steam.

Despite my best attempts, I hadn't been able to raise enough money to pay myself a living wage, let alone hire other staff. As a result, I'd been doing a lot of the heavy lifting myself, and that had taken its toll. I felt increasingly exhausted and frustrated. I desperately wanted to carry on, but simply couldn't.

Heartbroken, I went back to work at Jessica's Organic Farm while I decided what to do next. Before my resignation from Transition Sarasota,

Transition US had raised funds for me to travel to Northern California to facilitate a few workshops at the North American Permaculture Convergence. While my first instinct was to cancel, a friend encouraged me to go, saying: "Just see what happens." Once again, I packed my bags and headed out into the unknown.

Performing

Only after many rehearsals is the curtain ready to go up.
And still it evolves, but now with the added component
of the audience's energy and presence.

—Otto Scharmer, *Theory U* [10]

Performing isn't the culmination of our evolutionary journey as much as it's just one more stage in a never-ending spiral. Even though we may have achieved some measure of success, we can't simply rest on our laurels. Once we have reached the top of one hill, we can see there are even bigger mountains to climb off in the distance.

Nevertheless, through the process of Prototyping, we may eventually hit upon something that reliably works. Having attained this somewhat elevated state, we now have a responsibility to help guide others along the path, enabling them to come at least as far as we have, if not farther.

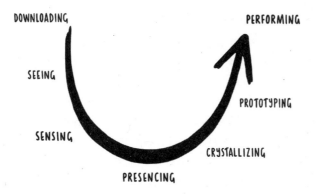

Figure 3.7: The seventh stage of Theory U.

The most important thing that happened while I was in California was that I reconnected with Carolyne Stayton, who was executive director of Transition US (TUS) at that time. We first met at a gathering of national Transition leaders that Michael Brownlee convened at Genesis Farm in New Jersey in 2009 and occasionally stayed in contact over the years. Since 2010, I'd worked with TUS in my capacity as a Transition Trainer, and became one of the first members of its national Collaborative Design Council in 2016.

When I floated the possibility of helping TUS revive its dormant training program, Carolyne suggested I become her co-director. Still recovering from burnout, I was taken aback by her generous offer, but said I'd seriously consider it. This was my dream job and a natural progression of the path I'd been on for the past decade. While it took a few months before I was ready to say yes, I started working for TUS in January 2017, helping to organize our first national conference.

I spent the next few years strengthening our relationships with local Transition Initiatives, revitalizing our training program, editing and publishing 10 *Stories of Transition in the US: Inspiring Examples of Community Resilience-Building*,[11] and producing dozens of online events, including our first online summit. With help from my friend and Transition Sarasota Board President, Roger Landry, I also started a small intentional community called the Novus House. Three friends and I tended a food forest and vegetable garden that took up the entire front yard, built a plant nursery and kept chickens out back, and transformed our swimming pool into a natural pond with fish and floating islands. We opened our doors for potlucks once a week, held regular house meetings, and organized community work days once a quarter.

Unfortunately, as time passed and members of our initial group left to pursue other opportunities, we found it difficult to attract new housemates who were knowledgeable and enthusiastic about intentional living. This was a new concept for Sarasota, and gradually, the Novus House turned into something I no longer wanted to be part of. In the middle of 2020, the first year of the pandemic, tired of living in Florida and able to work from anywhere, I decided to move back to Boulder.

Shortly after I arrived, Carolyne took her well-deserved retirement, and I became sole executive director of TUS. During that time, I focused on updating our internal systems, diversifying our staff and board of directors, expanding our budget, and providing additional support for local initiatives. That year, we held our largest leadership training ever, and in 2021, organized our biggest online conference, which was attended by over 1,100 people from all over the world.

In 2022, with TUS in a better place than it had been in years, I decided it would be a good time to take a sabbatical to finally write this book and pass the torch to new leadership. Currently, I'm living in another co-op here in Boulder and serving as Training Coordinator for the international Transition Network. Although I have some ideas about what might come next (including a land-based intentional community, demonstration site, and training center for the Transition Movement), I remain open to wherever my journey takes me.

The Transition Story

Just in case you were under the impression that Transition is a process defined by people who have all the answers, you need to be aware of a key fact. We truly don't know if this will work. Transition is a social experiment on a massive scale. What we are convinced of is this: if we wait for the governments, it'll be too little, too late; if we act as individuals, it'll be too little; but if we act as communities, it might just be enough, just in time.

— Transition Network, "The Cheerful Disclaimer"[1]

When the founders of Transition Town Totnes began their effort to build local community resilience and wean their small town off fossil fuels, they didn't expect to spark a global movement. However, because their approach proved so successful, it naturally spread: first to other cities and towns in England, then to the rest of the world.

Because Transition is so multifaceted, it can be difficult to summarize in just a few words. Perhaps its most concise definition comes from the international Transition Network, which describes it as "A movement of communities coming together to reimagine and rebuild our world." While this one sentence encompasses many key aspects of the Transition approach, it needs to be unpacked to be fully understood.

Unlike most movements that tend to focus on a single issue, Transition is exceptionally holistic. It seeks to address not only environmental concerns such as climate change and resource depletion but also a wide range of social and economic issues. Similarly, it seeks to transform not only

Table 4.1: Adapted from *The Transition Handbook* by Rob Hopkins.[2]

Conventional Activism	The Transition Approach
Single-issue	Holistic
Focused primarily on changing individual behavior or government policy	Focused primarily on inspiring collective action at the community level
Fighting the bad	Building the good
Primarily motivated by outrage	Primarily motivated by hope and possibility
Oppositional	Collaborative
Seeks to reform the current system	Seeks to foster a different way of life

external systems of food, energy, economy, and governance but also who we are as individuals and cultures. Because it's so holistic, there are many ways to get involved and everyone's invited.

Transition is primarily focused on creating change at the community level, not because individual and political transformation aren't important, but because so many other organizations and movements are already working on them. Acting locally is strategic because it's the scale at which most people feel they can make a significant impact. Acting collectively is strategic because it magnifies our efforts and helps participants feel less alone.

In terms of Joanna Macy's three-part framework,[3] Transition encourages a "paradigm shift" and supports "holding actions" that directly confront injustice, but is mostly concentrated on "building alternative structures" that embody the more just and regenerative world we want. Because of this positive and practical orientation, Transition tends to be motivated more by hope and possibility than driven by fear and anger.

Recognizing that we're all in this together, Transition also tends to be more collaborative than oppositional. Local Transition Initiatives partner with a wide range of other organizations, and Transition Hubs network these initiatives regionally, nationally, and internationally. Ultimately, Transition aims foster a different way of life that works for everyone, not merely reform the status quo.

All of this adds up to what's been called "The 'Transition Towns' Movement's Initial Genius."[4] While no one movement can hope to bring about all of the changes our world currently needs by itself, I believe Transition is an important piece of the puzzle. If it didn't already exist, someone would need to invent it.

Roots in Permaculture

For those who might be unfamiliar, Permaculture was cofounded in the 1970s in Australia by professor Bill Mollison and his then-student David Holmgren. Partly a response to the energy crisis of that time, they initially presented their work as an attempt to codify a "permanent agriculture," patterned after nature and Indigenous farming practices. In the decades since, Permaculture has expanded beyond this narrow definition and is currently understood to be a highly adaptable set of principles, skills, and solutions for creating a "permanent culture," one that's able to thrive indefinitely into the future without destroying humanity or the Earth.

Prior to founding the Transition Movement, Rob Hopkins was a Permaculture practitioner and teacher, teaching a two-year residential course in Practical Sustainability he'd created at Kinsale Further Education College in Ireland. His students learned about and practiced a wide array of regenerative skills including Permaculture design, organic gardening, field ecology, sustainable forestry, natural building, community leadership, social entrepreneurship, and conflict resolution.

As Hopkins tells it, the seed of the Transition Movement was planted during his travels to the Hunza Valley of Pakistan in 1990. Writing 16 years later in *The Transition Handbook*, he recalled what he observed and felt there:

> Here was a society which lived within its limits and had evolved a dazzlingly sophisticated yet simple way of doing so. All the waste, including human waste, was carefully composted and returned to the land. The terraces which had been built into the mountainsides over centuries were irrigated through a network of channels that brought mineral-rich water from the glacier above to the fields with astonishing precision.

Apricot trees were everywhere, as well as cherry, apple, almond and other fruit and nut trees. Around and beneath the trees grew potatoes, barley, wheat and other vegetables. The fields were orderly but not regimented. Plants grew in small blocks, rather than in huge monocultures. Being on the side of a mountain, I invariably had to walk up and down hills a great deal, and soon began to feel some of the fitness for which the people of Hunza are famed. The paths were lined with dry stone walls, and were designed for people and animals, not for cars.

People always seemed to have time to stop and talk to each other and spend time with the children who ran barefoot and dusty through the fields. Apricots were harvested and spread out to dry on the rooftops of the houses, a dazzling sight in the bright mountain sun. Buildings were built from locally-made mud bricks, warm in the winter and cool in the summer. And there was always the majestic splendor of the mountains towering above. Hunza is quite simply the most beautiful, tranquil, happy and abundant place I have ever visited, before or since.[5]

While Hunza may be where the seed of the Transition Movement was planted, it began to germinate in Kinsale. On the first day of the fall semester in 2004, Hopkins screened a documentary for his students that had recently been released called *The End of Suburbia*[6] and invited Colin Campbell, founder of the international Association for the Study of Peak Oil & Gas, to speak to them. While the information presented by Campbell and the film was deeply unsettling for both Hopkins and his students, it motivated them to look at how their own town might prepare for a future beyond fossil fuels.

The result of their explorations was *Kinsale 2021: An Energy Descent Action Plan*, which was published in 2005.[7] For each aspect of their local community, Hopkins and his students evaluated Kinsale's "baseline" resilience to peak oil and climate change, then laid out a "vision" for 2021. Finally, they engaged in "backcasting" to suggest what Kinsale would need to do each year in order to arrive at their vision on time.

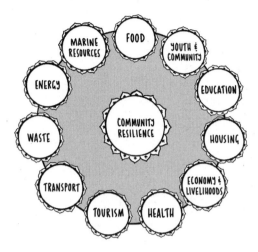

Figure 4.2: The Kinsale Energy Descent Action Plan, arranged as a mandala.

It's no coincidence that the topics explored in Kinsale's Energy Descent Action Plan bear a strong resemblance to the petals of the Permaculture Flower I mentioned in chapter 2. In *The Transition Handbook*, which was published only a few years later, Hopkins cited Permaculture as "one of the principal foundations of the Transition concept":

> When designing the transition that our settlements and communities will inevitably have to undertake, we need a design template with which we can successfully assemble its various components—social, economic, cultural and technical—in the most efficient way possible. Permaculture can be thought of as the design "glue" and the ethical foundations we use to underpin Transition work, to stick together all the elements of a post-peak settlement [...] Permaculture principles underpin this approach, which is designed to mainstream its concepts, presenting them as fundamental to any response to energy descent.[8]

Hopkins has even gone so far as to describe Transition as a form of "community-scale Permaculture." While many Permaculturalists also work for change at the community level, Permaculture's main focus, historically, has been on the scale of a single homestead, farm, or ecovillage.

Because *Kinsale 2021* was basically a student project, Hopkins didn't think too much of it at the time. However, after it was unanimously endorsed by Kinsale's Town Council and posted online, people all over the world started downloading it and contacting Hopkins to ask how they could do something similar. At that point, he had to say he didn't know because Kinsale's plan had been produced under such specific circumstances. Nevertheless, he would soon have an opportunity to prototype the process himself in another community just across the Irish Sea.

Transition Town Totnes

Later that same year, Hopkins moved with his family to Totnes, a small progressive town in South West England. Shortly after arriving, he met fellow sustainability educator Naresh Giangrande in a pub, and they decided to work together on what would become Transition Town Totnes (TTT). Their early successes inspired the formation of the Transition Movement and established a template for future Transition Initiatives to follow.

They started by setting up a steering group, a small team committed to helping TTT get up and running. This group began raising awareness by offering a series of talks and documentary film screenings that were designed to not only educate people about the "twin threats" of peak oil and climate change but also bring community members together to discuss how they might respond.

To lay the foundations for even broader-based support, TTT partnered with many local organizations over the years, including other nonprofits, schools, and local businesses. They built a bridge to local government and created events like Estates in Transition and an International Youth Music Festival specifically to connect with parts of their local community that were difficult to reach.

This prepared the ground for a Great Unleashing in September 2006. Introduced by the Mayor of Totnes and attended by more than 350 people (representing around 5 percent of their town's total population), it included keynote presentations, artistic performances, and an opportunity for participants to share their own visions for their community's future. The atmosphere was one of celebration, propelling TTT forward into its next phase of development.

Following their Unleashing, TTT hosted the first of several Open Space Days, using a format called Open Space Technology that facilitates self-organization around topics of common interest. This led to the formation of working groups focused on Food, Energy, Heart & Soul, the Arts in Transition, Economics & Livelihoods, Building & Housing, and Local Government. As these working groups started organizing their own awareness-raising events and launching their own practical projects, the steering group of TTT rebranded itself as a Project Support Group and expanded to include representatives from each working group.

Practical projects launched during this time included Oil Vulnerability Auditing, which trained participants to consult with local businesses to help them increase energy conservation and efficiency; the Totnes Renewable Energy Society, which catalyzed community investment in solar and wind; Totnes, the Nut Tree Capital of Britain, which planted dozens of fruit and nut trees throughout the town; and a Local Food Directory, which compiled information about all the local farms and farmers' markets in their area. The biggest project TTT established during these first few years was the Totnes Pound, a local complementary currency.

They also facilitated skill-building workshops under the banner of the Great Reskilling and sought to honor their elders by collecting oral histories. All of this was undertaken in the spirit of "letting it go where it wants to go," allowing the Transition process to unfold in an organic way.

In the fall of 2007, TTT began working on their Energy Descent Action Plan, which they eventually published as *Transition in Action* in 2010.[9] Around that same time, they also started exploring the possibility of redeveloping an abandoned industrial site in the heart of town, converting it into a center for local culture, affordable housing, and sustainable business.

The Viral Spread of the Movement

In 2007, with several groups throughout England and elsewhere already emulating the approach of Transition Town Totnes, the international Transition Network was established. The following year, Naresh Giangrande and Sophy Banks began offering the first Transition Trainings to support emerging leaders around the world, and Hopkins published his thoughts about this fledgling movement in *The Transition Handbook: From Oil Dependency to Local Resilience*, which quickly became a bestseller.

Since then, the Transition Movement has spread to over 1,000 communities in more than 50 countries.[10] Although it continues to be concentrated mostly in Western Europe and North America, Transition Initiatives also exist in Eastern Europe, Central and South America, Australia, Africa, Asia, and the Middle East.

Figure 4.3: Map of Transition Initiatives worldwide.

Transition has always encouraged initiatives to serve the needs of their local communities above all else. This means that every Transition Initiative is independent and autonomous, choosing how best to organize themselves, which topics to focus on, and which projects to undertake. Some focus primarily on growing their local food systems, while others dedicate their efforts to building more resilient local economies, transitioning off fossil fuels, or reducing consumption and waste. Many address a variety of these topics. Some attempt to tackle them all.

Although every Transition Initiative is unique, at least four things bind them together as a movement. One is a shared understanding of our global context. While there are differences within the movement about which issues are considered most important and how dire our predicament is, most Transitioners agree that modern civilization is fundamentally unsustainable and we need to act now to prepare for a future of escalating environmental, economic, and social crises. Exponential growth simply cannot continue indefinitely on a finite planet, and we're already beginning to experience the consequences of overshoot.

Another thread that connects Transition Initiatives everywhere is a common vision. Again, the details of this vision may vary from person to person and place to place, but the movement as a whole generally promotes the idea of relocalization. We envision and work towards cultivating more self-reliant, sustainable, and resilient local communities that are networked for mutual benefit. In a resource and climate-constrained future, we'll be forced to live closer to home, consume less, produce more of what we need locally, and cooperate with our fellow community members to get things done. However, if we prepare for this in advance, we might actually end up creating a more vibrant and equitable society, along with a better overall quality of life.

The third factor that broadly defines what Transition is and isn't is a set of guiding principles. The following eight are drawn from Transition Network's website, but the descriptions below are my own.

1. **We respect resource limits and create resilience:** Because we live on a planet whose abundant natural resources are rapidly being depleted, Transition advocates for dramatically reducing consumption to achieve sustainability. However, because we've already set in motion forces that threaten our communities, we also need to build resilience. While resilience is most commonly defined as the ability to bounce back from misfortune, it can also be thought of as a robust health and vitality that enables us to respond creatively to whatever challenges we might encounter.

2. **We promote inclusivity and social justice:** Transition strives to be as inclusive as possible not only because it's the right thing to do (which it is), but also because it makes us smarter and stronger. Transition requires an unprecedented coming together of society to be successful, so we need to intentionally cultivate all kinds of diversity in our movement: not only race and class but also age, gender, culture, sexual orientation, geography, and political affiliation. A commitment to social justice is likewise essential because strategies that fail to alter existing power dynamics and increase equality will not automatically lead to better outcomes for all.

3. **We adopt subsidiarity:** This principle means that Transition respects the autonomy of initiatives to decide what's best for themselves and their local communities. Transition Initiatives are always created by people who live in that place, are never required to pay dues, and don't even need to call themselves Transition Wherever. Because every community is different, imposing one-size-fits-all solutions would be counterproductive. Instead, regional, national, and international Transition Hubs exist to serve the grassroots movement, providing support for those engaged in practical action on the ground.

4. **We pay attention to balance:** Balance shows up in many different ways in the Transition Movement, but this principle specifically refers to a balance between the Head, Heart, and Hands of Transition. As well as seeking to understand our global predicament, we're actually doing something about it, not only in the external world but also internally, working to transform ourselves and our cultures.

5. **We are part of an experimental learning network:** From the beginning, it's been clear that there's no one right way to do Transition. Nevertheless, we can all benefit from sharing our experiences and insights with each other. By linking local, regional, and national groups together into a global network, we can more easily collaborate with each other, provide mutual support, and amplify our collective voice.

6. **We freely share ideas and power:** Whenever we discover a best practice or create a new resource, we're encouraged to share it with the rest of the movement. After all, none of us can afford to waste time reinventing the wheel. Transition groups at all levels are also encouraged to adopt and adapt democratic systems of governance that value the contributions of all members.

7. **We collaborate and look for synergies:** Transition groups regularly partner with a wide range of other organizations and institutions for mutual benefit. We don't try to pretend that we have all the answers or can fix everything ourselves. Because of this, Transition Initiatives and Hubs are exceptionally adept at weaving many disparate entities into a unified movement.

8. **We foster positive visioning and creativity:** While both utopian and apocalyptic visions of the future abound in popular culture, alternatives to the status quo that are plausible and attractive are precious and few. If we can't even imagine a better world, how can we hope to create one? Transition seeks to unleash the power of the imagination and the creativity of local communities to dream, design, and manifest their own destiny.

The Evolution of the Transition Model

The fourth factor that binds the Transition Movement together is its overall approach to changemaking. While Transition Initiatives are encouraged to experiment and discover what works best for them, having a model to fall back on can be extremely helpful when you don't know what else to do.

The Twelve Steps of Transition, as described by Rob Hopkins in *The Transition Handbook*, represent the first iteration of the Transition model. As you can see below, they were based largely on how the first few years of Transition Town Totnes unfolded. Although this model has been updated and revised multiple times, it remains probably the most well-known articulation of the Transition approach.

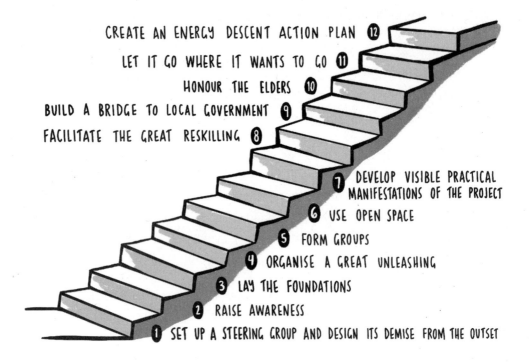

Figure 4.4: The Twelve Steps of Transition.

However, even as Hopkins was introducing his Twelve Steps to the world, he acknowledged they were really only an early sketch of the Transition process:

> These Twelve Steps emerged from observing how the Transition Town Totnes initiative evolved, and from other communities contacting us to ask what we were doing. They don't take you from A–Z, rather from A–C, which is as far as we've got with the model so far. These steps don't necessarily follow each other logically in the order they are set out here; every Transition initiative weaves a different way through the Steps, as you will see. These Twelve Steps are still evolving, in part shaped by your experience of using them. There may end up being as few as six or more than fifty![11]

In the first few years following the publication of *The Transition Handbook*, there wasn't any alternative to the Twelve Steps. As a result, they were taught around the world and reconfigured into a flow chart that was handed out to participants at introductory Training for Transition courses (now called Transition Launch Trainings). Simply referred to as "The Early Stages of Transition," this second iteration of the Transition model provided a slightly more nuanced look at how the Twelve Steps might be introduced over time:

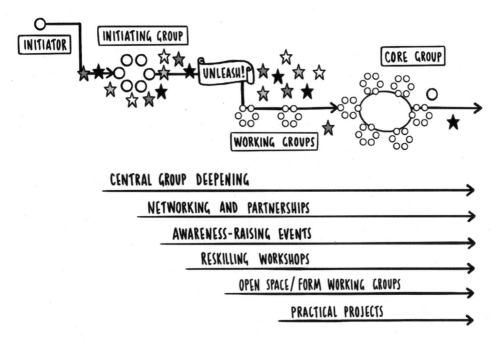

Figure 4.5: The Early Stages of Transition.

The Early Stages of Transition depict the journey of a single initiator who pulls together an Initiating Group, which subsequently engages in networking and partnering, offering awareness-raising events and reskilling workshops, and organizing a Great Unleashing. Following this Unleashing, the group begins to use Open Space Technology to catalyze the formation of Working Groups, which start organizing their own events and projects.

At this point, the Initiating Group morphs into a larger Core Group that includes representation from each of the Working Groups.

As the Transition Movement spread around the world to different countries and cultures, big cities and rural communities, neighborhoods and entire regions, Hopkins began to contemplate a third iteration of the Transition model. In an essay titled "Introducing a New Way of Understanding Transition" that was circulated prior to Transition Network's 2010 international conference, Hopkins announced his intention to "throw the whole model in the air":

> Why might we need to rethink the way we conceive of what Transition is, and how we communicate it to others? The 12 Steps, or 12 Ingredients of Transition, have been, until now, how we communicate what Transition is, and how it works. But over time, it has become increasingly redundant, as Transition becomes a broader, deeper and more complex model [...] Also, one gets the sense sometimes that some would have it that the 12 Steps were carried down from Totnes Castle carved on tablets of stone by a man with a long white beard. In planning for the second edition of *The Transition Handbook*, the temptation became overwhelming to throw the whole model in the air and present it in a completely different way.[12]

This "completely different way" was eventually presented by Hopkins in his 2011 book, *The Transition Companion: Making Your Community More Resilient in Uncertain Times*.[13] However, before that, he posted draft versions of each section in serial to his now-defunct blog, *Transition Culture*, where he invited Transitioners from all over the world to provide suggestions and feedback. Many did, helping to refine Hopkins' original ideas and make them more applicable to a wider variety of contexts.

Although Hopkins initially referred to *The Transition Companion* as a pattern language, he abandoned this term after being told it was too esoteric for most people to grasp. Instead, he ended up presenting this first major update to the Transition model as a set of interconnected Ingredients and Tools, loosely organized into five developmental stages. In contrast to *The Transition Handbook*, which was a massive hit, response to *The Transition Companion* could be categorized as lukewarm at best.

I believe there are a few reasons *The Transition Companion* was largely overlooked at that time. Mostly, it was just way too complex: its 43 Ingredients and 21 Tools were much harder to wrap one's head around and remember than the Twelve Steps. Also, the difference between Ingredients and Tools wasn't always clear, and the stages they were sorted into often seemed arbitrary.

In 2012, I was introduced to a fourth iteration of the Transition model. At that time, it was referred to as the Transition Dog, but was later renamed the Transition Animal. While a few different versions currently exist, mine is based primarily on the "7 essential Ingredients for doing Transition successfully" outlined in Transition Network's *Essential Guide to Doing Transition*.[14] The main point of the Transition Animal is to identify the essential ingredients of Transition and show how they all need to work together like parts of a single body.

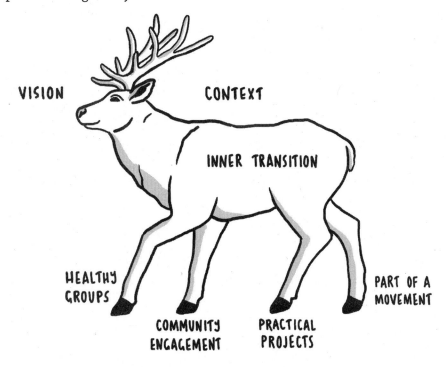

Figure 4.6: The author's version of the Transition Animal.

In chapter 2, I categorized the Transition Animal as a pattern of Wholeness. As such, it incorporates all of the key elements related to the horizontal dimension of Transition, but doesn't speak to its vertical dimension: how these elements transform and evolve over time. For example, the kinds of practical projects that initiatives are able to accomplish later in the Transition process are often impossible at the beginning. For a detailed understanding of how we get from here to there, we need to look elsewhere.

The Five Stages of Transition

A journey from one place to another can take a number of different routes, but will usually pass through a series of distinctly different landscapes. You don't necessarily notice when you leave one and enter another, but there are moments when you realise you are in a very different place. The Transition journey is similar. You find that you move from raising awareness, showing films and trying to interest people, to noticing that you seem to have created an organisation that has different needs from those it had originally, and then later starting to think about what new businesses and infrastructure your community needs. Each stage is like finding yourself in a distinct landscape.

— Rob Hopkins, *The Transition Companion*[1]

Like all things, Transition must continually evolve or else stagnate and decay. However, unless its evolution is rooted in its past and the hard-won wisdom of those working on the ground at the local level, it could easily become untethered, jumping around from big idea to big idea without ever really landing anywhere. For this reason, any attempt to shape Transition's future needs to walk a fine line between innovation and continuity, tradition and transformation.

As mentioned in the previous chapter, the Five Stages of Transition emerged out of a collaborative process Rob Hopkins facilitated with Transitioners around the world and served as the overarching framework for his *Transition Companion*. As such, the Five Stages are firmly rooted in

Transition's past. On the other hand, he only wrote a few sentences about each of the stages themselves, and it wasn't always clear why he assigned Ingredients and Tools to the stages he did. As a result, the Five Stages as described in *The Transition Companion* could be considered another early sketch of a model, one that still needs to be fleshed out.

Like many others, I was somewhat put off by the complexity of *The Transition Companion* at first. Nevertheless, knowing Hopkins' penchant for brilliance and how this book had been written, I suspected I was missing something important. As a result, I returned to *The Transition Companion* again and again, seeking to uncover its essence. Doing so, I began to observe a close correlation between the Five Stages and my work with Transition Sarasota, which didn't appear to be merely coincidental.

Eventually, I came to understand the Five Stages as a remarkably accurate description of how the Transition process naturally unfolds, rather than some arbitrary theory Hopkins dreamed up on his own. We begin by trying out our best ideas and seeing what sticks (Starting Out), then focus on what's working and pare away the rest (Deepening). This prepares the ground to reach beyond the usual suspects (Connecting), which, in turn, enables us to transform entire systems and sectors (Building). Finally, by networking many impactful local initiatives together, we can begin to exert real influence at national and global levels (Daring to Dream).

Working through each of the first four stages creates the necessary conditions to open a door to the next, leading towards the kind of widespread transformation the Transition Movement has long envisioned but has yet to achieve. In total, the Five Stages present a realistic pathway for deepening, broadening, and scaling up the impact of any Transition group.

This vertical perspective has been mostly lacking in Transition so far. While the movement continues to grow and some initiatives have accomplished truly amazing feats, the majority seem stuck in its early stages: raising awareness, partnering with like-minded organizations, and running a few small projects. While this is obviously better than nothing and nobody is being forced to scale up, I believe it's only by doing so that we will fundamentally change the world.

The Five Stages are a pattern that incorporates elements of both Transformation and Expansion. While they align with the trajectory of the U, they also ripple outward from the individual to the group to the community to the world. Weaving these two aspects of the Five Stages together with Hopkins' metaphor of a journey through a series of distinct landscapes, I've concluded the best way to depict them is as a spiral path leading up from a valley into the foothills and eventually to a mountainous peak:

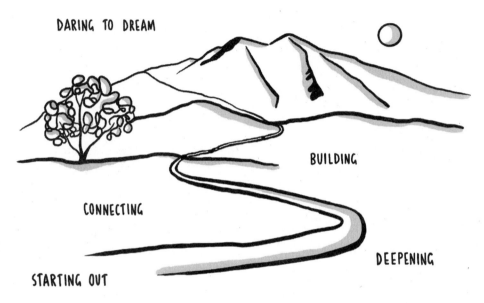

Figure 5.1: The Five Stages of Transition, depicted as a mountainous journey.

My approach in this chapter will be to set aside the 64 Tools and Ingredients of *The Transition Companion* to focus on the Five Stages themselves. In the following sections, I will walk you through each of the stages as I understand them, describing their essence and key features and sharing examples from my work with Transition Sarasota to illustrate each one. By doing so, I hope to show that the Five Stages can serve as a reliable map, not only for Transition Initiatives but for changemaking efforts of all kinds, enabling leaders to identify where they currently are and figure out what's next.

Starting Out

These first ingredients take you from Transition being just an idea or an aspiration to its being something that is under way with a good chance of success.

— Rob Hopkins, *The Transition Companion*[2]

Starting Out typically begins with one person or a few people who find out about Transition and become deeply inspired by it. They might read a book, then take a training and decide to form an Initiating Group. To recruit additional members, they might reach out individually to people they already know or organize a public event to pitch the Transition concept and find out who else might be interested.

Once established, Initiating Groups are encouraged to take however much time is needed for members to get to know each other, discuss how they'll work together, and develop shared purpose. After that, the group is ready to pick a name and have a logo designed, set up their website and newsletter, and begin raising awareness.

Awareness-raising events serve several important functions. They help to not only educate people about your initiative and provide opportunities for partnership but also build community and generate ideas for action.

STARTING OUT

Figure 5.2: The first stage of Transition.

When you're just Starting Out, it might not be clear yet what will and won't resonate with your community, so it makes sense to experiment with a variety of topics and formats to see what draws the most interest.

Most importantly, awareness-raising events establish a base of support for the initiative's further development. By connecting with those who show up, listening to their feedback, and offering opportunities for them to become more deeply involved, we begin to open a door to Deepening.

In 2010, soon after establishing an Initiating Group for Transition Sarasota, we started organizing awareness-raising events. Our first effort was a documentary series called *Five Films for a Future*. Thanks to support from the Sarasota Friends Meeting House (where the screenings were initially held), WSLR 96.5 FM (our community radio station), and the Peace Education & Action Center (another local nonprofit), we packed the house with nearly 100 people the first night. Even more attended subsequent screenings, which generated a powerful sense of momentum.

As word spread, I began receiving unsolicited invitations from a wide variety of local groups, from the Rotary Club to the Sierra Club, to speak about Transition at their meetings and conferences. We also started tabling regularly at community events and organized reskilling workshops on herbal medicine, backyard biodiesel, organic gardening, solar cooking, and Nonviolent Communication. As a result, our email list quickly grew to more than 1,000 subscribers. Everything seemed to be going great, until that initial burst of excitement started to peter out.

Deepening

Your Transition initiative will build momentum and practical projects will start to emerge. You may have to design for the sustaining of the organisation and the deepening of its work, broadening engagement across the community and being more efficient and effective.

— Rob Hopkins, *The Transition Companion*[3]

At a certain point, simply raising awareness is no longer enough. When you begin to notice the same old people are showing up to your events, having the same old conversations, that's a sure sign that it's time to shift into Deepening.

Of course, you can choose to ignore this signal and keep doing what you've done before, but if you do, your supporters will gradually lose interest and drift away. I've heard many organizers complain they can't get anybody to come to their meetings or fill leadership positions anymore, but there's usually a good reason for that. People need to feel their time is being well-spent and that your group at least has the potential to accomplish something meaningful. Without a continual sense of forward momentum, most understandably give up.

Deepening means becoming more focused, effective, and impactful. Now that you've tried out your brightest ideas and observed your community's reaction, you can learn from that and adjust your approach accordingly. This requires ruthlessly paring away what isn't working to concentrate on what is. Generally, it's more strategic to do just a few things with excellence than a bunch of things halfway.

Drawing on the base of support and partnerships you cultivated during the Starting Out stage, you can now begin moving into action. At this stage, projects should be relatively small and manageable. If they're too big, they can overwhelm your group's capacity and make it impossible for you to do anything else. Starting small also increases your chances of success and enables you to fine-tune as you go. Once you have a prototype dialed in, you can always scale it up.

To support practical projects of any size, it's usually necessary to incorporate as a formal organization. Although most Transition Initiatives start as all-volunteer groups with little to no funding, those that stay that way tend not to accomplish much or last very long. Without a board of directors and staff to coordinate the initiative as a whole, volunteers burn out and eventually no one is left holding the center. As Henry David Thoreau wrote in *Walden*: "If you have built castles in the air, your work need not be lost; that is where they should be. Now put the foundations under them."[4]

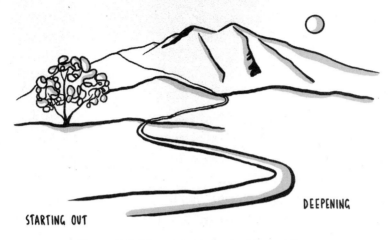

STARTING OUT

DEEPENING

Figure 5.3: The second stage of Transition.

For its first five years, Transition Sarasota enjoyed the fiscal sponsorship of the Peace Education & Action Center. In exchange for a modest percentage of our overall revenue, their board of directors served as ours, handled all of our paperwork, and enabled us to fundraise legally. Due largely to the fact that we were one of the only Transition Initiatives in the US at that time to have full-time staff, Transition Sarasota quickly became known as one of the most active and impactful groups in the country.

Our first practical project was the Suncoast Gleaning Project. During the six and a half years I served as Transition Sarasota's executive director, we harvested more than 250,000 pounds of organic produce from local farms that would have otherwise been wasted and donated it to local food banks to benefit the food insecure in our community. This project was absolutely pivotal in Transition Sarasota's development, as it engaged hundreds of volunteers and demonstrated we could make a real difference. It was a positive, photogenic story that attracted a lot of media attention. Everyone could easily see its value.

This marked the beginning of Transition Sarasota focusing almost exclusively on local food. While we might have concentrated on zero waste or renewable energy instead, we decided to focus on food because there was already so much interest in it. We knew we couldn't do everything and wanted to make a significant impact in at least one area. If we could achieve that, it would send a powerful message about our ability to transform all of the other aspects of our community as well.

Connecting

It is often said that the scale of a proper response to peak oil and climate change would be akin to the preparations for the Second World War. Every aspect of our lives needs to turn on a sixpence, in a coordinated and effective way. The ingredients in this section explore how Transition initiatives can play a part in that process, and take Transition to a wider audience.

— Rob Hopkins, *The Transition Companion*[5]

While the Transition process is about connecting from the very beginning, in the Starting Out and Deepening stages, we're mostly connecting with like-minded individuals and forming partnerships with like-minded groups. Until we've demonstrated that our initiative can make a real impact, more mainstream individuals and institutions are likely to be hesitant to engage.

However, once we've proven ourselves and built a reputable organization, we're in a much better position to reach beyond the choir and cultivate relationships with local businesses, media outlets, foundations, and government agencies. This is what is meant by Connecting.

Working Groups become an essential strategy at this point. They enable more and more people to step into leadership roles and expand an initiative's capacity beyond what can be managed by one small circle. As these groups generate more and more of their own events and projects, the role of those stewarding the initiative as a whole naturally shifts from driving it forward to supporting what's emerging.

Other possibilities that begin to present themselves at this stage include establishing coalitions and running multifaceted campaigns. While no one initiative can hope to transition an entire community by itself, a movement of diverse stakeholders united by a common purpose stands a much better chance.

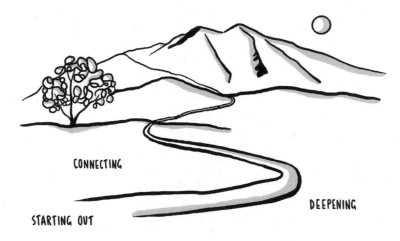

CONNECTING

DEEPENING

STARTING OUT

Figure 5.4: The third stage of Transition.

Although Transition Sarasota reached out to many potential partners early on, only those that were already ideologically aligned with us were even willing to give us the time of day. However, once we started donating tens of thousands of pounds of produce every year to feed the hungry, organizations that had previously given us the cold shoulder came knocking. As a result, our funding and capacity increased and other groups began looking to us to serve as a focal point for the local food movement in our community.

In 2011, we launched our online Eat Local Resource Guide & Directory alongside our first annual Eat Local Week. For more than a decade now, Eat Local Week has brought together dozens of partners to offer dozens of fun and educational events celebrating the best of local food and farming in Sarasota and Manatee counties. Our Eat Local Guide, which began with only 97 listings, grew over the next five years to include more than 260 related businesses and organizations and was eventually distributed as a print publication. These two projects both helped to foster a much more interconnected and powerful local food movement.

At this point, we started to merge all of our activities into an overarching Local Food Shift Campaign, organized around a central goal of shifting Sarasota County food purchases at least 10 percent towards local sources. According to a 2006 study by Ken Meter of the Crossroads Resource Center,[6] this had the potential to add at least $80 million per year to Sarasota

County's economy and create thousands of new green jobs. To facilitate this, we invited individuals and organizations to sign a 10 percent Local Food Shift Pledge and encouraged our city and county governments to do the same.

Building

Transition groups aim ultimately to catalyse the localisation of their local economy. They strive to move from running small community projects to thinking and acting much bigger. New skills and ways of thinking will lead Transition initiatives to become social enterprises, such as becoming developers, banks, energy companies, and so on.

— Rob Hopkins, *The Transition Companion*[7]

Having established a base of support in Starting Out, strengthened your initiative's foundations through Deepening, and expanded your reach and capacity through Connecting, you finally have everything you need to accomplish the really big projects your group initially came together to do. These might be things like running a regional food hub, coordinating a local currency, or setting up a community-owned renewable energy company. While some Transition Initiatives attempt to implement system-changing strategies like these earlier on, without the support, resources, and expertise developed through Starting Out, Deepening, and Connecting, they are rarely successful.

One example of this is creating an Energy Descent Action Plan. It takes a huge amount of time, energy, and/or resources to establish an accurate baseline for an entire community and produce a detailed vision with actionable steps. Even if you can produce the plan, if you haven't already cultivated widespread and enthusiastic support for the ideas in it, it will likely end up gathering dust on a shelf somewhere instead of being implemented in any meaningful way.

From the beginning of the Transition process, strategy is essential to make the best use of limited resources and capacity. However, it takes on a different meaning at this stage. When you're just Starting Out, you have to be at least somewhat opportunistic. Now that you have more freedom to pick and choose which projects to undertake in which order, you also have a greater responsibility to thoughtfully prioritize what your community needs most.

Much of what is needed in the Building stage revolves around local economic development: encouraging people to invest in local businesses, catalyzing social entrepreneurship, and creating dignified livelihoods that further sustainability and justice. As long as most people are spending 40 hours a week working for companies that are actively pushing our world in the wrong direction, a Great Transition won't be possible. Charity alone can't fix all of the problems we're facing. We need an entirely different economy that places people and planet above profit, thrives on cooperation rather than competition, and provides most of what we need much closer to home.

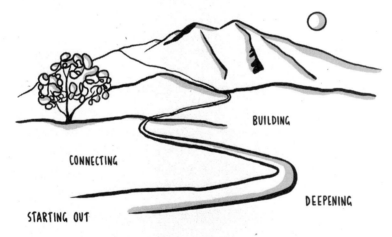

Figure 5.5: The fourth stage of Transition.

Recognizing a need to continue to scale up and building on everything we'd already done, Transition Sarasota's next step was to demonstrate that local food could be a powerful strategy for economic development. Towards that end, we began partnering with Slow Money, an international network of groups facilitating investment in local food enterprises. In 2013, we brought Slow Money founder Woody Tasch to Sarasota as our Eat Local Week keynote speaker, and subsequently organized two Local Food Entrepreneur Showcases that introduced potential investors to businesses seeking investment.

We also explored commissioning a new local food study from economist Michael Shuman, setting up a hub for the aggregation and distribution of local produce, and establishing a certification and branding scheme for local food businesses. However, due to a lack of funding and capacity, these Building projects have yet to come to fruition.

This is an important point. If we find ourselves trying to move forward into the next stage but not having much luck, we'd be smart to look back and ask ourselves what work we might still need to do in earlier stages to advance. When I left Transition Sarasota, I'd say we were on the cusp of Building, but needed to develop ourselves more in Connecting first. In retrospect, I think we needed to educate more people about these unfamiliar ideas, build stronger relationships with local foundations, and hire more staff to effectively manage these projects.

Daring to Dream

The old saying "Think global, act local" is still relevant. The ingredients and tools included in the sections so far in this book, if implemented, will create a groundswell for change; a catalyst for communities around the world to see an energy-constrained future as the motivator for creative change, rather than as a disaster. But without Transition thinking being embraced by national government and business, and becoming central to the national infrastructure, it will remain marginal.

— Rob Hopkins, *The Transition Companion*[8]

When Hopkins initially outlined the Five Stages of Transition, this final stage was the most opaque. There were only three Ingredients assigned to it ("Policies for Transition," "A learning network," and "Investing in Transition"), and it wasn't entirely clear how they were supposed to be connected. Nevertheless, the short paragraph Hopkins wrote to introduce Daring to Dream, which is quoted above, summarizes it well. It's about the movement as a whole stepping up to national and international stages, becoming a force to be reckoned with, and actually changing the world.

Having contemplated this for years now, I've come to believe that the only way the Transition Movement will achieve this level of power and influence is by helping enough Transition Initiatives move through the Starting Out, Deepening, and Connecting stages to thrive at the Building stage. If we're able to network hundreds or thousands of these Building initiatives together, we'll be able to prove Transition really works, not just a little in some places but a lot in many different contexts. At that point, it might be possible to break through to a much larger world of high-profile partnerships, major government and foundation support, national and international media attention, and real political power. This will only happen, though, if we're able to show Transition is significantly improving people's lives and solving pressing problems on the ground. A flashy PR campaign, by itself, won't cut it.

Do we dare to envision a future in which Transition is debated as vigorously by politicians and the mainstream media as taxes, guns, immigration, and abortion? The fate of modern civilization is at least as important as these other issues. Can we imagine a time when billions of people are actively involved in the work of regeneration? As absurd as it might seem right now that we could actually accomplish this, this is what our world is asking of us. It's also what Transition has been aiming at all along.

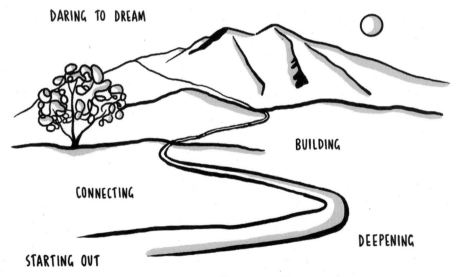

Figure 5.6: The fifth stage of Transition.

The Five Stages of Transition demonstrate how one person with no funding, special connections, or prior experience can start a local initiative and end up changing the world. As remarkable as that is, they mainly address only the vertical dimension of the Transition process. To form a more complete model, the Five Stages need to be cross-referenced and integrated with the Seven Essential Ingredients of Transition. This will be the focus of the next seven chapters.

Our Global Context

History, Stephen said, is a nightmare
from which I am trying to awake.

— James Joyce, *Ulysses*[1]

As unpleasant as it is, we need to be willing to bear witness to the suffering of our world if we want to help change it. Without an accurate understanding of history and the most powerful forces shaping our present, we have little hope of bringing about a better future. The visions we hold and the actions we take are inevitably shaped by our understanding of context.

It's also important that we're able to talk knowledgeably about the reasons why we're doing what we're doing. This doesn't mean we all have to become experts in multiple fields or memorize an endless array of statistics, but we do need to seek out information from reputable sources and consider a diversity of perspectives to avoid being duped by false narratives and half-truths. If we fail to do our due diligence, that will greatly undermine our credibility as leaders.

Because sharing information about the state of our world can be deeply disturbing for those who haven't fully reckoned with it yet, we should be careful about how we do this. It's always wise to speak from the heart, be honest about what you know and what you don't, refrain from beating people over the head with what they already know, and provide ample space for them to process what's been said. We should also always do our best to connect problems to solutions and suggest ways that people can take action. We have a responsibility not to leave others to figure everything out on their own.

Usually, when people feel they're being attacked, they entrench more deeply in their existing positions. For this reason, it's generally more effective to simply state what you believe, allow others to do the same, and enter into dialogue rather than try to convince anyone of anything. We can see and speak to general trends, but our world is far too complex to predict specific events with any precision. When in doubt, it's best to err on the side of humility. As Nobel Prize-winning physicist Nils Bohr famously quipped: "Predictions are difficult, especially about the future."

Even before I started writing this chapter, I knew it would be foolish to try to summarize every issue facing humanity in just a few short pages. So instead of attempting to provide a comprehensive account of our global context, I've chosen to focus on one particular throughline: how the pursuit of endless exponential growth has begun to run up against natural limits, and how that, in turn, is likely to impact our economy and society as a whole.

Other writers have chosen to frame our current context differently. James Howard Kunstler titled his seminal work *The Long Emergency*,[2] and Richard Heinberg coined the phrase "peak everything"[3] to refer to the converging crises of the twenty-first century. Joanna Macy speaks of the "Great Unraveling" of the "Industrial Growth Society," and the Movement Generation Justice & Ecology Project points to the "Extractive Economy"[4] as the source of persistent injustice and environmental degradation.

This version of the story starts in 1972, when MIT systems analysts Donella and Dennis Meadows, Jørgen Randers, William Behrens, and others published a groundbreaking report called *The Limits to Growth*.[5] Analyzing a series of computer simulations based on five main variables (population, food production, industrialization, pollution, and nonrenewable resource consumption), they concluded that, without a major course correction, the global economy would begin colliding with Earth's natural limits sometime between 2010 and 2020. Although *The Limits to Growth* caused a huge amount of controversy when it was first released, its predictions have since been found to be remarkably prescient.[6]

The idea that limits to growth exist should be obvious. A finite Earth simply cannot sustain more and more people consuming more and more all the time. However, because modern civilization has become so deeply habituated to and dependent on growth, very few (especially those in the mainstream media and politicians of all stripes) have the courage to question it. In fact, the doctrine that growth is always necessary and good may be as close to a universal religion as we have in this day and age. Even Bernie Sanders would dare not broach this taboo, lest he be run out of Vermont on a rail.

Growth is good up to a point, but beyond that, it becomes a cancer. Humanity's relentless pursuit of endless growth is particularly dangerous because it happens to be exponential in nature. We typically think about growth as a gradual, linear process (one becomes two, two becomes three, and three becomes four), but anything that grows by a consistent percentage multiplies and compounds over time (4 becomes 16, 16 becomes 256, and 256 becomes 65,536). Even as the rate of change remains constant, the amount of change increases dramatically. This is why the late Al Bartlett used to say: "The greatest shortcoming of the human race is our inability to understand the exponential function."[7] Because exponential growth starts slow before rapidly accelerating, it has the ability to confound our expectations and catch us by surprise.

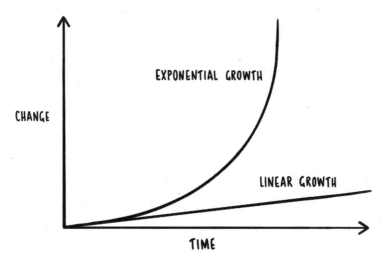

Figure 6.1: Two kinds of growth.

We could use this same generic exponential growth curve to describe the trajectory of just about every aspect of our world over the past 10,000 years. From seemingly benign developments like growth in human population and Gross Domestic Product to more obviously undesirable ones like biodiversity loss, resource depletion, and global warming, change itself has been speeding up: more and more, bigger and bigger, faster and faster. This helps explain why life feels like it's becoming increasingly complex, stressful, and chaotic.

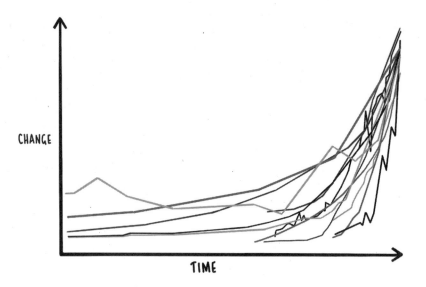

Figure 6.2: Many growth curves, all rising exponentially.

All of this raises some very important questions: how long can we continue in this direction before we simply can't grow anymore? When that happens, how will it impact our lives? And, given the massive scale, urgency, and apparent intractability of the challenges we're facing, is it still possible to turn things around in time?

Environmental Crisis

Transition was initially described as a new kind of environmental movement, focused primarily on responding to peak oil and climate change. Over the past two decades, even as climate change has become a more clear and present danger, concerns about peak oil have receded into the background.

There are good reasons for this. Although the International Energy Agency confirmed in 2010 that conventional oil production had peaked in 2006[8] and record-high oil prices in 2008 likely played some role in triggering the Great Recession, the cataclysmic effects that many peak oil analysts predicted never materialized.

This was due, in large part, to a subsequent influx of investment capital into the production of what are commonly referred to as "unconventional" fossil fuels: fracked gas, shale oil, tar sands, and deepwater drilling. While many analysts foresaw this, it was definitely not a welcome development. Unconventional fossil fuels not only tend to cost more to produce than their conventional counterparts, they also typically generate higher greenhouse gas emissions and cause much more environmental damage.

Around that same time, an influential article by 350.org founder Bill McKibben[9] pointed out that to stay below 2°C of warming, humanity could only afford to release an additional 562 gigatons of CO_2 into our atmosphere. However, corporations and national governments already had 2,795 gigatons listed as proven reserves on their balance sheets. This meant that to avoid catastrophic climate change, we would need to find a way to keep more than four-fifths of the world's remaining fossil fuels, worth tens of trillions of dollars, permanently in the ground.

This will be even more difficult than most people think. The generally agreed-upon "safe" limit of warming is now 1.5°C, and we have already passed 1.2°C.[10] Despite knowing this, global emissions continue to rise every year.[11] Although many countries, states, cities, and corporations have pledged dramatic action by 2030 or 2050, it's too soon to tell yet whether they will actually follow through. According to a 2021 investigation by the *Washington Post*,[12] less than half of all countries, representing only 30 percent of global emissions, had submitted updates required by the 2015 Paris Agreement. This same article revealed that many of these reports had greatly underestimated emissions while overstating the impact of carbon sequestration efforts.

To complicate matters further, the climate crisis is unlikely to be solved by simply switching out fossil fuels for renewable energies. In a 2010 book, analysts from the Stanford Research Institute calculated what it would take to replace the cubic mile of oil the world was consuming every year at that time.[13] They found that we would need to install a mind-boggling 91,000,000 solar panels or 33,000 giant wind turbines every year for 50 years merely to replace oil (not counting coal or gas). Although deployment of wind and solar technologies has greatly accelerated in recent years, they still only supply about 10 percent of the world's total energy consumption.[14]

Compared to fossil fuels, which are reliable, energy-dense, and relatively easy to transport, solar and wind energies are intermittent, diffuse, and costly to store or transmit over long distances. To use renewables as our main source of power, we'll have to rebuild our entire energy infrastructure. Many of the materials required to make solar panels, wind turbines, and batteries are also rare, depend on hugely destructive mining operations, and cannot yet be recycled. This isn't to say that we shouldn't increase renewable energy production as fast as we possibly can, but it's definitely not the silver bullet solution many have been led to believe.

Furthermore, one gallon of gasoline contains the same amount of energy as 500 hours of hard human labor, and every time we turn on a 100-watt light bulb, it's as if a cyclist is pedaling as hard as they can just to keep that bulb lit. The average US household employs the equivalent of 50 such cyclists around the clock.[15] Knowing this, it's easy to understand how fossil fuels have so profoundly transformed our world in just a few short centuries and how losing them (through depletion or regulation) is likely to impact society.

However, we don't seem to have much of a choice. We're already experiencing more frequent and powerful heat waves, droughts, wildfires, storms, and floods. Additional warming will intensify all of these trends and risk tipping our climate into a runaway state where positive feedback loops could make it impossible for humanity to rein in further warming. This could lead to coastal cities sinking into the sea, persistent crop failures and mass migrations, tropical diseases spreading to formerly temperate areas, and so many supercharged natural disasters that we may find ourselves unable to fully recover from the last one before the next one hits. If we continue down this path, we could end up creating a planet that's fundamentally inhospitable to life for thousands of years to come.

Economic Contraction

As the cost of responding to these escalating disasters continues to increase and climate change compels a rapid transition away from fossil fuels, this will obviously have far-reaching effects on our global economy. Because the price of energy is embedded in the cost of almost everything, aggressive policies to curb emissions and rely increasingly on less profitable renewable sources will make it more and more difficult to sustain economic growth.

Unfortunately, our economic system has been designed in such a way that it must continuously expand or else collapse. For example, US dollars, which currently serve as the world's reserve currency, are created in one of two ways: as Federal Reserve notes, which are exchanged for Treasury Bonds and spent into existence, or as computerized loans, which banks essentially create out of thin air whenever they lend money. Because every dollar in circulation is owed back to somebody with interest, when defaults begin, they can easily domino, cascading throughout the global economy.[16]

Since the New Deal helped to end the Great Depression here in the US, we've learned that with enough government spending, we can arrest a downward spiral, as we did somewhat successfully in 2008 and 2020. However, as costs increase and growth stalls, this may no longer be possible. As of August 2023, US federal government debt had reached nearly $33 trillion, up more than $27 trillion since the turn of the century.[17] While we can currently borrow as much as we need at reasonable rates because lenders are still confident they'll get their money back, what happens when their faith begins to crumble? At that point, we'll only have a few options: spend less (cutting budgets), tax more (burdening taxpayers), default on our obligations (provoking conflict with creditors), or print more money (causing inflation).

A similar dynamic is at play in the stock market, where a loss of confidence in future growth could easily topple this particularly fragile house of cards. Currently, the financial sector is valued at $22.5 trillion globally, representing a quarter of all economic activity.[18] However, unlike the real economy of goods and services, the financial economy could evaporate virtually overnight, making it much more difficult to access capital. This would lead many businesses to stop investing in themselves, decrease production, downsize their workforces, and eventually go bankrupt.

Our economy has become abstracted to the point of absurdity. Those who grow our food, without which we would not survive, tend to be compensated poorly, while investment bankers are paid millions and billions. Countries frequently import the same amount of a given product as they export and sickness contributes more to GDP than health. Everything is upside down.

While we desperately need a different economic paradigm, agriculture offers a potent example of how difficult transitioning to a truly sustainable economy will be. Our heavily industrialized system of food production, which is responsible for 10 percent of US greenhouse gas emissions,[19] is extremely vulnerable to a decline in the availability of cheap fossil fuels. Massive amounts of oil are necessary to power the heavy machinery required for factory farming, and natural gas is needed to produce the synthetic fertilizers farmers depend on to grow crops in long-abused and degraded soil.

A shift to small-scale, diversified, regenerative farming and local food systems will also take a lot more work. Based on the experience of Cuba, which was forced to rapidly transition its system of industrial agriculture following the collapse of the Soviet Union, Post Carbon Institute Senior Fellow Richard Heinberg has calculated that, without fossil fuels, the US would need approximately 50 million farmers to feed itself.[20] Currently, there are only 3.4 million farmers in the US, and their average age is 57.[21]

How will we convince tens of millions of young people to enter a profession that's incredibly demanding and, at present, not very lucrative? We can't wait to make this transition until market pressures or a major food crisis compels us. It'll likely take decades to train new farmers, reallocate land, rebuild degraded soils, and re-establish local and regional distribution networks. Systems change isn't nearly as simple as flipping a switch, and similar obstacles will need to be overcome in other sectors.

Social Chaos

How we choose to respond to environmental crisis and economic contraction will have at least as much of an impact on our collective future as these forces themselves. Joanna Macy has said the reason she created the Work That Reconnects is "so when times get tough, people don't turn against each other."[22] If we turn towards each other, I don't think there's anything we can't overcome. However, if we panic and blame each other for our predicament, that will just make everything else we have to do harder.

Although much progress remains to be made, many important advances towards a more just and equitable society have occurred within the past few centuries. Feudalism is no longer the norm, genocide and slavery have been outlawed, respect for human rights has become more widespread, and diversity is often celebrated as a strength. Nevertheless, we have to consider whether this trend might slow, stall, or even reverse course in our twenty-first century context of the limits to growth.

Developments here in the US and globally in recent years seem to suggest that it could. While contemporary social issues like political polarization, a resurgence of authoritarianism, racism, and xenophobia, and a proliferation of conspiracy theories, mass shootings, and mental illness may seem unrelated to deteriorating environmental and economic conditions, these conditions might actually be a large part of what's driving them.

I don't think most people are oblivious to the state of our world, despite appearances to the contrary. I believe everyone knows in their heart of hearts that the jig is up, even if they don't understand exactly why or what they might do about it. As a result, some lash out and grab at power, while others lose themselves in elaborate fantasies or succumb to cynicism, apathy, and despair.

If we consider the coronavirus pandemic as a test of how we might respond to even greater crises ahead, we'd have to say the results were mixed at best. Even though it was widely known that climate change, the growth of cities, and more frequent international travel have made pandemics much more likely, governments were still caught off guard. I know I was when the lockdowns began. I certainly didn't expect we'd still be struggling with COVID-19 more than three and a half years later and that over seven million people would die worldwide.[23]

Towards the beginning of the pandemic, most people responded admirably, as they often do in the adrenaline-fueled early days of a crisis. We set up mutual aid networks, sang to each other from balconies, and applauded the heroic efforts of health care workers. Everyone sacrificed to help "flatten the curve," and many were inspired to learn how to grow their own food. As supermarket shelves emptied, seed sales went through the roof. Of course, some hoarded toilet paper and hand sanitizer, but overall, in the first months of the pandemic, there was a massive upwelling of compassionate action and community spirit. In *A Paradise Built in Hell: The Extraordinary Communities That Arise in Disaster*, Rebecca Solnit refers to this phenomenon as "disaster collectivism."[24]

This was on full display about two months into the pandemic, when Minneapolis police officers were captured on video murdering George Floyd in broad daylight. Although police killings of Black men in the US weren't anything new, the Black Lives Matter movement was suddenly thrust into the spotlight, and protests surged to unprecedented levels. This created favorable conditions for a deep and widespread reckoning with American history, white privilege, systemic racism, and the militarization of policing.

Some important reforms were passed as a result, but over time, momentum for change began to dissipate. Similarly, our collective resolve to prioritize the health and safety of the most vulnerable weakened as calls to reopen schools and economies grew louder. Wild conspiracy theories like QAnon started popping up everywhere, and mental illness, especially among children, skyrocketed.[25] Even seemingly uncontroversial acts, such as wearing a mask or getting a shot to protect against a deadly illness, became highly politicized and contentious.

While Donald Trump deserves his fair share of the blame for the especially nasty turn the pandemic took here in the US, it's important to remember he was elected by 63 million people who knew exactly who they were voting for. Trump has always been a selfish, greedy, unrepentant con man with racist and authoritarian tendencies. That he lied and bungled his way through this crisis, used it as a pretext to push through xenophobic policies, and cheered on white supremacists as they stormed state capitols brandishing Confederate flags and semi-automatic weapons shouldn't have surprised anyone.

All of this culminated in the attack on the US Capitol on January 6, 2021. Although it initially appeared to be a spontaneous insurrection, since then it's become clear that it was actually part of a multifaceted plan to overturn the election. Despite this being the first attempted coup in US history, its leader has yet to be imprisoned and is currently running away with the Republican nomination for president.

We need transformational leadership at the top, but it's not clear that people here in the US are ready for that. Instead of nominating a progressive like Bernie Sanders or Elizabeth Warren or Cory Booker in 2020, Democratic voters chose the most moderate candidate available: Joe Biden. What the Democratic majority wanted wasn't radical change but simply a return to "normal."

If I'm correct in my assessment that social chaos has intensified in recent years at least partly due to a widespread sense of impending doom, we can only imagine what we might experience in the future, when even

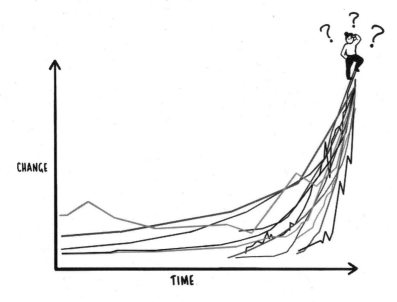

Figure 6.3: "Where do we go from here?"

more frequent and destructive climate disasters are occurring in the midst of a permanent economic recession. My nightmare scenario is that a smarter, savvier version of Donald Trump will rise to prominence out of this growing chaos. This is why I tend to worry even more about how society will respond to the Great Unraveling than I do about the environmental and economic trends that are precipitating it.

As dire and disturbing as our global context currently is, it's important to remember that humanity has overcome existential crises before and its resilience should never be underestimated. Probability isn't destiny, and necessity is the most powerful motivator of all.

Personally, I still have hope. Not hope that all of our problems will be solved by a charismatic leader, technological breakthrough, or mass awakening. It isn't even hope that we'll somehow escape the consequences of our historical karma and everything will work out in the end. It's a hope that's rooted in my experience of the power of people, communities, and movements to create our world anew. As long as we can still envision a better future, we still have a chance to realize it.

The Power of Vision

Where there is no vision, the people perish.

—Proverbs 29:18[1]

Harnessing the power of positive vision has been an important part of the Transition approach from the very beginning. While many organizations and movements hold a piece of the overall puzzle, Transition is one of only a few that I'm aware of that fits them all together.

It does this by flipping our usual way of thinking on its head. Instead of seeing our global predicament purely as a problem, we could embrace it as a historic opportunity for regeneration. In a sidebar to *The Transition Handbook* titled "Is 'peak' oil really the most useful way of looking at this?" Rob Hopkins flips M. King Hubbert's infamous graph[2] upside down to reveal a more hopeful vision for life after fossil fuels.

> When we look at the standard Hubbert curve, we see a mountain: a rise followed by a fall, an ascent followed by a descent. There is a sense that we have reached the peak and that now we have to grit our teeth for the long journey home, akin to an overexcited child at a birthday party being told it is time to go home. Perhaps the sense that we need to instill could come from turning this much-viewed graphic upside down. We might more usefully use the term "trough oil."
>
> Rather than a mountain, we could view the fossil fuel age as a fetid lagoon into which we have dived. We had been told that great fortunes lay buried at the bottom of the lagoon if only we were able to

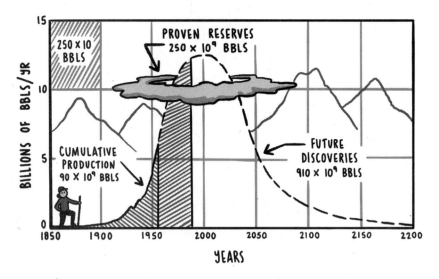

Figure 7.1: Hubbert's peak.

dive deeply enough to find them. As time has passed, we have dived deeper and deeper, into thicker, blacker, stickier liquid, and now we find ourselves hitting against the bottom, pushing our endurance to the extreme, surrounded by revolting sticky tar sands—the scrapings of the fossil fuel barrel. We can just about see sunlight still glinting through the liquid above us, and our desperate urge to fill our lungs begins to propel us back upward, striving for oxygen.

Rather than being dragged every step of the way, we propel ourselves with focused urgency towards sunlight and fresh air. Viewed like this, the race for a decarbonised, fossil fuel-free world becomes an instinctive rush to mass self-preservation, a collective abandonment of a way of living that no longer makes us happy, driven by the urge to fill our lungs with something as yet not completely defined, yet which we instinctively know will make us happier than what we have now. Perhaps arriving in a powered-down world will have the same sense of nourishment and elation as finally breaking through the surface and filling our lungs with fresh morning air, marvelling once again at the beauty around us and the joy of being alive.[3]

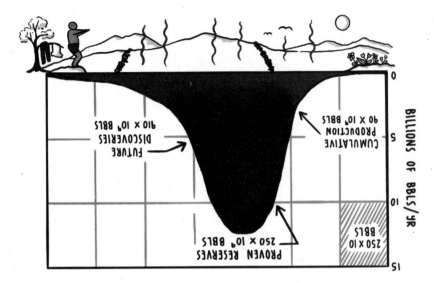

Figure 7.2: Trough oil.

While it's important that we don't fall into the trap of naive utopianism, there's obviously some truth in what Hopkins is saying here. We don't live in the best of all possible worlds, and a simpler life lived with greater integrity and purpose might actually be preferable to the one we have now.

As previously mentioned, the Transition vision is organized around the concept of relocalization. This is not to say that globalization is all bad. I believe the unprecedented degree of cross-cultural exchange it has enabled has been positive on the whole for humanity, and I hope that can continue. However, because economic globalization now threatens our very survival, it needs to be reversed.

Even though it has some obvious downsides, a relocalized, regenerative future might actually offer greater benefits. It might bring communities closer together and return power to the people to decide their own destiny. At least here in the developed world, it might involve less work, affording us more time to spend with our families and pursue creative interests. It might also encourage us to be more compassionate with each other and feel better about ourselves, which would be no small thing.

For a vision to capture our imagination and move us to action, it needs to show us a future worth working for, not just ways to do less bad. Fortunately, cities that are walkable, bikeable, and busable, with lots of open space, unique local businesses, and vibrant culture are among the most desirable places to live. Countries like Denmark, Costa Rica, and Bhutan that have chosen to prioritize quality of life and environmental protection over economic growth are also consistently ranked among the happiest in the world.[4] As humans, we are evolutionarily predisposed to these kinds of places and a slower, simpler, more natural way of life. Most of us don't thrive on speed and stress, concrete and chemicals, isolation, abstraction, and long hours spent staring at screens.

Nevertheless, a vision also needs to be realistic. If it isn't, it's a dangerous distraction. While the Transition vision may seem far-fetched, there's nothing fundamentally impossible about people banding together to create largely self-sufficient, sustainable, and resilient local communities. In fact, we've already done that for thousands of years. It doesn't require a major technological breakthrough, divine intervention, or the subversion of any laws of nature.

Most activist groups post a vision statement to their websites, but vision has so much more potential as a tool for transformation. It can be used to enliven the ways we communicate as well as the design of our projects and events. We can create art that imagines what a Great Transition might look like, help others envision the future for themselves, and weave individual visions into a shared narrative. We can choose to place vision at the center of everything we do.[5]

Although the Transition vision remains relatively unknown, I believe it's only a matter of time before that changes. As the Great Unraveling becomes increasingly apparent, more and more people will start seeking out alternatives to the status quo. At that point, we will need a vision that can rally many different people together and inspire humanity to rise to the challenges of our times.

Jesus Christ's "Kingdom of God," the "more perfect union" of the US Constitution, and Dr. Martin Luther King Jr.'s "Beloved Community" are all visions we can draw on for inspiration, but who has vision in these times? In my experience, corporate and political leaders, and even most in the non-profit sector, do not. More of the same, only better, does not qualify as a compelling and realistic vision. If we have a contest of visions, I think ours wins.

I personally can't think of anything more worth dedicating my life to than Hopkins' vision of "an economic, cultural and social renaissance the likes of which we have never seen," in which we will see "a flourishing of local businesses, local skills and solutions, and a flowering of ingenuity and creativity."[6] While people will always choose to live in different ways, the Transition vision makes plenty of room for everyone.

No one can claim to know the future. Nevertheless, visioning remains a valuable practice. It helps us think through potential scenarios and responses, sharpening our understanding of the present while strengthening our readiness for what's still to come. In the following sections, I'll describe a couple of different ways to think about our future, then guide you through an exercise designed to help you envision it for yourself.

Future Scenarios

One of the most useful frameworks I've found for thinking about what our collective future might hold is David Holmgren's *Future Scenarios*.[7] Each line in the illustration below represents global trends in population, energy and resource use, and pollution and waste. On its left side is yet another representation of the story of exponential growth I told in the previous chapter, referred to here as Industrial Ascent. On its right are the shapes of four potential scenarios that might unfold over the next several hundred years.

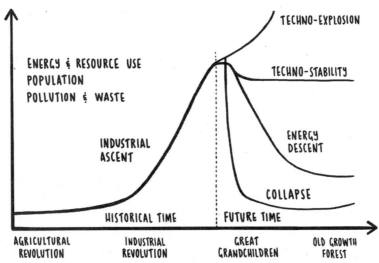

Figure 7.3: David Holmgren's Future Scenarios.

Before we turn to look at the individual scenarios, however, it's important to recognize they aren't mutually exclusive. In fact, they all exist in some form in our world today and will continue to exist, to a greater or lesser extent, in the future. To emphasize this point, Holmgen quotes the science fiction writer William Gibson, who observed: "The future is already here. It's just not evenly distributed." The first three scenarios are familiar to most people, while the fourth remains mostly unknown.

Techno-Explosion: In an earlier iteration of this model, Holmgren didn't disguise his scorn for this scenario, labeling it the "Techno-Fantasy." Nevertheless, it continues to prove compelling for many. Popular sci-fi visions from *The Jetsons* to *Star Trek* have long promised better living through technology and greater adventure among the stars, in which we can leave our troubled lives and world behind.

While appropriate technology will certainly play a role in the Great Transition, betting the future of human civilization on speculative breakthroughs like nuclear fusion or carbon capture and storage is a gamble I don't think we can afford to make. Even if they somehow happen, new technologies often create more problems than they solve. One example of this is the enthusiasm with which many people living in big cities in the early twentieth century greeted the arrival of the private automobile. While cars did save them from the scourge of horse manure piling up in their streets, we now know that the internal combustion engine has created a different pollution problem many orders of magnitude worse. This same specter of unintended consequences hangs over proposed present-day technological fixes such as artificial intelligence and geoengineering, both of which are rapidly gaining popularity.

Perhaps the epitome of the Techno-Fantasy is the billionaire's race to space. I'd love to ask Elon Musk specifically how he plans to colonize Mars, down to the smallest detail. Even if he's able to muster the resources and technological wizardry to do so, wouldn't his efforts be better focused here on Earth? Compared with the dusty desolation of Mars, Earth is still a veritable Garden of Eden. We already have a breathable atmosphere, soils that grow crops, forests and oceans, and millions of species of bacteria, fungi, plants, and animals that have co-evolved over billions of years.

Collapse: Many people in war-torn regions and failed states are already living through a form of Collapse, and it isn't unthinkable that more might be joining them soon. The recent ubiquitousness of apocalyptic novels, movies, and TV shows seems to me a sign that even people in relatively stable and wealthy countries are beginning to contemplate this possibility.

There are some I know who welcome Collapse as a way to wake people up and start over with a clean slate, but this is a very dangerous idea. We are nowhere near prepared for this. If modern civilization collapsed tomorrow, billions would suffer and likely die for lack of access to food, money, and health care. It would be an unprecedented disaster. While I agree we shouldn't waste much time or energy trying to prop up an outdated and exploitative system, we do need time to develop alternatives at scale.

In a context where Collapse is an increasing possibility, "prepping" by learning how to grow one's own food and gathering essential supplies to weather an emergency is obviously prudent. However, building bunkers and stockpiling guns and ammo seems to me a distraction from the work of building resilient communities. I, for one, don't want to spend my precious time preparing to live underground on a ruined Earth or training to kill my hungry neighbors. In a Collapse scenario, we'll either thrive together or suffer apart.

Techno-Stability: If you look closely at Holmgren's diagram, you'll see that the lines for the Techno-Explosion and Collapse scenarios actually run together at first, as do those for Techno-Stability and Energy Descent. This is intentional. The brief overlap between Techno-Explosion and Collapse is meant to signify that continuing to push growth too far beyond its limits will result in a precipitous crash. The slightly longer overlap between Techno-Stability and Energy Descent suggests the possibility that these two scenarios may appear indistinguishable for a time, but will eventually diverge as more radical change becomes unavoidable.

Techno-Stability is essentially the belief that incremental reform of current systems is a sufficient response to our predicament. I remember watching *An Inconvenient Truth*[8] when it first came out and being shocked when, after an hour and a half of listening to Al Gore prophesize the end of the world, most of the solutions superimposed over the credits were things like switching out your light bulbs, bringing reusable bags to the grocery store, and buying electric cars. Despite these suggestions being utterly inadequate to the crisis at hand, they're still the kinds of responses most often promoted by people in positions of power.

While taking small steps towards sustainability by doing things like recycling and taking shorter showers is important, if that's all we do, it won't be nearly enough. If we believe we can keep consuming as much as we want and flying all over the world as long as we purchase "green" products and carbon offsets, we won't fundamentally change the way we live. Similarly, if we think governments and corporations will solve all of our problems for us, we aren't likely to engage in collective action. To respond to our global predicament with the seriousness it requires, we need to move beyond Techno-Stability as well.

Energy Descent: It's not hard to see why this fourth and final scenario is almost entirely absent from mainstream political discourse. Mere mention of the possibility of descent is considered heresy by those who still worship at the altar of endless expansion. Although I believe Energy Descent is our most realistic and hopeful option, it points in exactly the opposite direction from the path humanity as a whole has been pursuing.

One common criticism of Energy Descent is that its proponents want to take us back to the Stone Age. However, this is an extreme misrepresentation. At least in the short term, Energy Descent will likely look a lot more like the first half of the twentieth century here in the US than hunting squirrels and living in caves.

It's also important to recognize that, compared to Collapse, Energy Descent would be much more gradual and likely bottom out at a higher level. In his 2009 book, *The Ecotechnic Future*, John Michael Greer suggests four broad stages civilization might pass through over the next several centuries: "the end of affluence," "the age of scarcity industrialism," "the age of salvage," and "the coming of the ecotechnic age."[9] Although Greer studiously avoids making specific predictions about what this ecotechnic age might look like, its name alone suggests the possibility that, even hundreds of years from now, we might be able to maintain some of what's best about modernity.

While some movements, like Permaculture and Transition, have explicitly framed their work as a response to this Energy Descent scenario, its ethos of learning to do more with less is the implicit motivation behind many other changemaking efforts, such as those focused on growing local food systems, strengthening local economies, increasing energy conservation and efficiency, and achieving zero waste.

Energy Descent can also be seen as a manifestation of the meta-pattern of Transformation. If we flip Industrial Ascent and Energy Decent upside down, they clearly form a U. Over the past 10,000 years, more and more people have begun Seeing and Sensing the downsides of humanity's obsession with endless growth, conquest, and domination, which has led us to a point of collective Presencing. Now, we can hopefully start Crystallizing, Prototyping, and Performing new ways of living in harmony with nature and each other that serve to regenerate the whole.

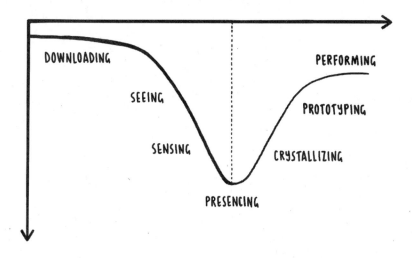

Figure 7.4: Industrial Ascent and Energy Descent
as a manifestation of Theory U.

Although Energy Descent requires a reduction in overall rates of resource extraction and consumption, it doesn't necessitate a similar decline in quality of life. In fact, if we engage in it proactively, cooperatively, and creatively, we might actually find our world becoming a more pleasant place to live. Throughout this process, we'll need to rewrite the definitions of some of our most cherished values (such as freedom, prosperity, and progress), but we don't need to abandon them altogether.

A Just Transition

The term "just transition" was originally created by organized labor to refer to the need to support workers whose jobs have been lost or are threatened because of the transition to renewable energy. However, in recent years, it has also been used more broadly by organizations like the Climate Justice Alliance and the Indigenous Environmental Network to refer to the need for justice to shape every aspect of the Great Transition. In their influential zine, *From Banks and Tanks to Cooperation and Caring: A Strategic Framework for a Just Transition*, Movement Generation powerfully asserts that while "Transition is inevitable. Justice is not."[10]

Although Energy Descent suggests the possibility of creating a more equitable society, it isn't automatically just. It's entirely possible that we could solve the climate crisis while making current injustices and inequalities even worse. This potential dark side of Energy Descent includes eco-fascism, in which authoritarian governments impose harsh restrictions in the name of survival, and what I have come to call "transition apartheid," where rich people retreat to their fortified, off-grid mansions while those who can't afford expensive new technologies are left to struggle with increasing levels of deprivation.

To avoid these ghoulish scenarios and advance equity and justice through the Great Transition, at least two big things need to happen.

1. Those who have benefitted the most from Industrial Ascent need to dramatically reduce consumption while helping others raise their standard of living: Although this would have been much easier to accomplish in an era of economic expansion than it will be in a degrowth future, equality remains a moral imperative. Even in times of dwindling resources, we have to ensure that everyone has at least their basic needs met. Economist Kate Raworth points to the possibility of bringing everyone into a "safe and just space for humanity" between our "ecological ceiling" and a non-negotiable "social foundation."[11]

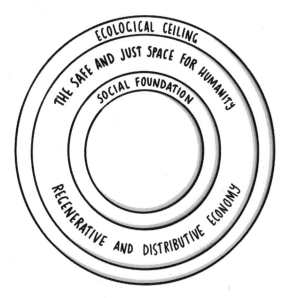

Figure 7.5: Doughnut Economics.

2. The solutions that are implemented in response to the Great Unraveling need to be intentionally designed to further justice: For example, if we try to reduce greenhouse gas emissions primarily by building industrial-scale solar and wind farms that are owned and operated by private corporations, we'll end up reinforcing and exacerbating inequality. However, if we focus instead on retrofitting homes and buildings for maximum efficiency, investing in public transportation, and connecting rooftop solar arrays into community-owned micro-grids, we can reduce our dependence on fossil fuels and lower greenhouse gas emissions while meaningfully shifting the current balance of wealth and power.

One of the most compelling visions of a just transition I've seen is the short animated video, *A Message from the Future*, which was produced by Congresswoman Alexandria Ocasio-Cortez, illustrator Molly Crabapple, author Naomi Klein, and The Intercept in 2019.[12] Movement Generation's Just Transition Framework similarly envisions a regenerative future underpinned by a commitment to "Caring & Sacredness," "Deep Democracy," "Cooperation," and "Ecological & Social Well-Being."[13]

Clearly, it isn't enough to "just" transition: how we transition matters. We need to not only secure a livable world for future generations but also protect those who are most vulnerable right now. By standing together on the common ground of justice, we could actually bring about a better world for everyone.

Visioning a Post-Transition World

Now that we've taken a hard look at our global context, surveyed a wide range of potential futures, and considered the importance of a just transition, I'd like to share an exercise designed to help you develop your own vision. Called "Visioning a Post-Transition World," it was originally developed by Sophy Banks and continues to be taught all over the world as part of Transition Launch.

I've edited Banks' script somewhat and adapted it for this book, but my version remains close to the original. Visioning a Post-Transition World walks you through a day at some undefined point in the future when the Great Transition has actually occurred. Everything isn't perfect, but life is generally better than it was, and humanity is beginning to get a handle on its biggest existential issues. This activity is an opportunity to envision what that world might look like, sound like, feel like, and be like, down to its most intimate details.

To begin with, find yourself a quiet place where you won't be interrupted and set aside at least 30 minutes for this exercise. You could read the following inset text to yourself or ask somebody to read it (slowly) to you. What's most important is that you don't try to control your experience. Just observe whatever happens to come to mind without judgment. You might be surprised by what you discover.

> Please take your seat and sit up as straight as you comfortably can. Rest your hands face down on your thighs and place your feet flat on the floor. Now, close your eyes. Begin to tune into your breath as it flows in and out through your nostrils, slightly cool on the inbreath and slightly warm on the outbreath. Then, slowly scan your body for any areas of tension and allow them to gradually melt away.

Finally, look at your mind. Is it busy or peaceful, steady or agitated? Give yourself permission to let go of any thoughts that may still be pinballing around in your brain so they can dissolve completely into openness.

We're now going to embark on a journey together to a post-transition world, to a possible future for you and your community. Imagine that you fall asleep in your bed tonight, and while you're sleeping, a miracle occurs. You are transported forward in time to a day when the Great Transition has more or less happened. The changes that are needed for a just, sustainable, and regenerative human presence on the planet are already well underway, and you're about to wake up in this future world.

When you open your eyes in this world, what's the first thing you see? What is this place where you've been sleeping? Allow yourself to look around and notice every detail as you're waking up. What is the quality of the light? Do you hear any sounds, smell any smells?

After a few minutes, you roll out of bed and start to get dressed. What are you wearing? How does it feel on your skin? Let your imagination show you how you get ready for your day in this post-transition world.

At some point, you notice you're hungry and go to find something to eat. Where do you do that? Where does your food come from? Is anyone there with you? If so, who? What are you eating, and how does it taste? Do you have anything to drink with your meal? If so, where does that come from? What do you talk about or think about over breakfast?

Now it's time to start your day's activity. Again, don't try to control this. Just observe whatever arises. What do you do for work? Is it one thing or several? Do you need to travel to your workplace, or do you work from home? If you need to travel, how do you get there and what's that like?

Do you work by yourself or with others? If you work with others, who are they and what are they like? What's your workplace like, and how's it organized? What kinds of conversations, if any, do you have? What do you do all day, and how does it feel?

Time has passed in this future world, and you've now come to evening. Imagine yourself going to some kind of gathering or celebration. Where is this held? What are you doing? Who's there with you, and what's it like? How does it feel to be part of this community? What brings you joy?

Let time flow forward again until it's time to go home. At this point, stop and look back at your community and the nature that surrounds it. What do you observe? What do you hear? How does the air smell and taste? How are you feeling at the end of your day in this post-transition world? What do you dream of? What do you hope for?

Your day in this post-transition world is now coming to an end. You're back in bed, about to fall asleep. In your sleep, you drift backwards in time, knowing you can revisit this place any time you want.

When you're ready to come back, start by feeling your weight on your chair and the sensations of your body. Then, take a few last deep breaths and gently open your eyes.

Once you've returned from this post-transition world, pick up a pen and paper and take as much time as you want to write and reflect on what you've just experienced. If you're part of a group, you might encourage others to do this exercise as well and exchange visions afterwards. You might even plan to revisit this activity periodically to track how your visions evolve.

Envisioning 2050

Because I try to always practice what I preach by only preaching what I practice, I've decided to share with you my vision for 2050. I chose to focus on the half-century mark because it's a time that isn't too far away to relate to but is still distant enough to allow for significant transformation to occur. It also happens that 2050 is the year by which climate scientists have said we need to achieve net zero greenhouse gas emissions, so this vision can be seen as a contemplation of what that might look like as well.

The future I envision is not without its challenges, but it's one in which our difficulties have brought us closer together. Many of the things we used to think were so important no longer have such a grip on us. In the face of climate chaos, energy descent, and economic contraction, our perspective has shifted. We've come to value time over money, relationships over things, quality over quantity, and community over convenience. Most of the time, we're simply trying to figure out how to live. Nevertheless, there's much joy and beauty to be found along the way.

In 2050, I imagine myself living just outside of Boulder, Colorado, on a 25-acre intentional community, regenerative farm, and educational center that my partner and I cofounded over two decades ago. Although we met too late to have kids, the community we built together has come to feel like family. Currently, two dozen of us live and work on the land: some single people, some couples and families; all ages, genders, colors, and creeds.

The land itself is mostly flat and forested, with a large pond and a drainage ditch, screened from the main road by a row of majestic cottonwoods. When we purchased it, a four-bedroom house and a barn were already on the property. Over the years, residents have built various smaller houses, cabins, and yurts for themselves using cob and strawbale techniques. All of these structures are clustered towards the front of the property around a central green space with a playground and community garden plots for everyone.

Towards the back, seven and a half acres are devoted to regenerative farming. There are two large greenhouses, a food forest with dozens of different kinds of fruit and nut trees interspersed with perennial vegetables and herbs, a large market garden with annual row crops, and a menagerie of honeybees, chickens, and goats. Community members maintain it all by hand. Even though our fields are blanketed with smoke from nearby wildfires almost every summer, we still manage to produce nearly all of what we eat, fill a few dozen Community Supported Agriculture shares, and stock our booth at the downtown farmers' market twice a week. We trade with other local farms for things we don't grow (like meat and grains) and occasionally buy items we can't produce in our climate (like coffee and chocolate).

In the late 2020s, strict rationing of water from the Colorado River and Ogallala Aquifer was instituted due to persistent drought. Around that same time, restrictions on rainwater harvesting were finally lifted. Like many of our neighbors, we now depend on several thousand-gallon cisterns to meet most of our needs. On the farm, we use drip irrigation to maximize efficiency and reuse greywater as much as possible. We've also installed composting toilets in every building. We simply can't afford to waste anything anymore.

Solar panels mounted on every south-facing rooftop are connected to batteries that provide power when the sun isn't shining. While these panels don't produce nearly as much energy as we were used to before fossil fuels were banned, we've learned to get by on much less. We now wake up with the sun and go to bed when it's dark, spend most of our time outside, and use electronic appliances and devices sparingly. Gone are the days of streaming Netflix all night and posting pictures of our food on social media. Now, we use the internet mostly to check the news and weather and stay in touch with family. All of our buildings have been highly insulated, so they can be kept warm throughout the winter by small stoves fueled by wood pellets pressed onsite.

Each house is owned individually, but all other structures and the land itself is held in common by a community land trust, which is managed by a board of directors that includes representatives from every household and volunteers who represent the interests of our wider community. We meet once a month in our glass and timber-framed common house to review financials, discuss current challenges, and make decisions that affect the community as a whole. Issues that only affect residents are discussed at weekly community meetings.

Everyone who is physically able to works on the farm and helps to run our educational programs. We regularly offer classes, weekend workshops, and longer courses in Permaculture gardening and farming, bioremediation, sustainable forestry, natural building, renewable energy systems, meditation and yoga, herbal medicine, cooperative governance, Transition-style organizing, and social entrepreneurship. Many of us also have side hustles, both on and off the land. At 68, I'm mostly retired from farmwork but still teach, serve on the Boulder County Commission, and occasionally consult for neighboring communities.

All of this keeps us so busy that we don't leave the community much except to go to market, run errands, and occasionally retreat to the mountains and hot springs. For these trips, we use a communal pickup and a large van, both converted to run on biodiesel from a nearby farm. Most of our free time is spent much closer to home: sharing meals, going on hikes, playing games, and making music together. A few times a year, we invite our friends, students, and customers to the farm for a bonfire, potluck, and jam session. These seasonal celebrations lift our spirits and give us something to look forward to throughout the year.

On the rare occasions I venture into the city, I'm reminded of how much Boulder has changed. The most obvious feature is there's now food growing everywhere: in front yards and backyards, along every street, on former sports fields and in public parks. To ensure that no one goes hungry, produce is gleaned from local farms and community garden plots are made available for those who don't have access to land. School gardens teach kids valuable skills and supply their cafeterias. Growing food is no longer a niche pastime. It has become a critically important economic strategy.

Very few new homes have been built since the mid-2030s. To accommodate a growing population of climate refugees and uphold our commitment to ending homelessness, zoning codes have been updated and relaxed. People now generally live much more closely together, with extended families moving back in and co-ops taking over what were formerly single-family homes. Accessory dwelling units have come to populate nearly every backyard. Due to this increased density, neighborhoods have become much more vibrant places. Neighbors know each other, frequently share with each other, and occasionally throw block parties in the streets.

Most of Boulder's electricity comes from rooftop solar, but a few community-owned solar and wind farms have been built in rural areas to supply additional power to the local grid. Since almost everyone gets around now by foot, bike, and public transit, there's much less traffic and the air is cleaner. We can once again see the stars at night and hear birdsong in the city. A decade ago, the entire downtown area was closed to cars. Cafe tables now fill the empty streets where people gather late into the night. Murals and other art installations can be found on nearly every block.

As the global economy faltered, many large corporations and businesses that couldn't adapt ended up failing. Some big-box stores and warehouses were razed for urban and suburban farms, while others were repurposed for housing and light manufacturing, community centers and indoor markets. Most of the abandoned storefronts downtown have been taken over by local entrepreneurs, who regularly trade with each other. Many are cooperatively owned, and all are required to pay a living wage. Dollars are still exchanged, but Boulder Bucks are the preferred currency, as they can be spent almost everywhere.

The University of Colorado, which used to serve upward of 40,000 students, has shrunk to a fraction of its previous size. At the same time, community colleges and technical schools have enjoyed a renaissance. Overall, learning tends to be a lot more experiential and less abstract these days. Reading, writing, and arithmetic are still taught, but there's a much greater emphasis on their practical applications. Apprenticeships are once again the primary form of on-the-job training.

Because many more people now work outside with their hands, eat an all-organic plant-based diet, and receive greater support from their community, mental and physical illnesses have declined precipitously. Hospitals still provide surgeries and prescribe pharmaceuticals when necessary, but herbal medicines and alternative therapies are much more common. Homebirths and at-home hospice care have become the norm, increasing demand for midwives and doulas.

State, national, and international governments continue to exist, but due to a lack of funding and capacity, their role in society has diminished. As a result, local governments and civic organizations have been forced to take on a lot more responsibility. Because people can more easily see the impact of their actions on the local level, they're generally more politically engaged.

During my time on the County Commission, I've pushed to harness our collective intelligence through citizens' assemblies and participatory budgeting processes. Out of this has come a number of initiatives, including universal rights to food, housing, health care, and employment; a climate refugee resettlement program; a revolving loan fund for social enterprises; increased funding for restorative justice; and a set of community resilience indicators we track and regularly report on.

Overall, we've been extremely lucky here. I know others haven't been quite as fortunate. Even considering Boulder's many advantages, I couldn't have imagined back in 2024 how well we'd be faring. In fact, I'm exceedingly proud of all we've already accomplished together, and I've never been so hopeful about our collective future.

Inner Transition

*If you want to solve the world's problems, you have to put
your own household, your own individual life, in order first.
That is somewhat of a paradox. People have a genuine desire to
go beyond their individual, cramped lives to benefit the world.
But if you don't start at home, then you have no hope
of helping the world.*

— Chögyam Trungpa, *Shambhala: The Sacred Path of the Warrior* [1]

When Rob Hopkins and Naresh Giangrande started Transition Town Totnes, they had no plan to include inner work as part of their community-based response to peak oil and climate change. Why would they? They were starting a local sustainability initiative, after all, not a church.

However, after attending one of their first events, which she later said promoted "a fairly dim view of what humans are like," ecopsychologist Hilary Prentice decided to reach out to Hopkins to advocate for the importance of integrating the Inner Transition. To her surprise, he immediately suggested she convene a working group to explore this topic with others. The resulting "Heart and Soul Group" was hugely popular, which led to similar groups forming around the world and to the Inner Transition eventually becoming an essential ingredient of the Transition model. [2]

Although this joining of inner and outer in Transition may seem inevitable in retrospect, it wasn't. Communities of faith have often been at the forefront of successful movements, but it's still rare for secular activist groups to incorporate psychological insights into their work or encourage the spiritual development of their members. To be sure, there are compelling reasons why most activist groups choose to avoid this particular territory: it's deeply personal and fraught with potential pitfalls. Nevertheless, I believe that Transition's embrace of the inner has only made it stronger.

Fundamentally, the Inner Transition isn't anything mysterious or esoteric. Groups and movements are made up of people who have thoughts, feelings, values, and beliefs that shape how they perceive and interact with their world. The cultures they create likewise influence their collective priorities, strategies, and success. Understood in this way, paying attention to our own internal dynamics is indispensable for bringing about the change we want to see in our world.

This point might be further clarified by taking a closer look at integral philosopher Ken Wilber's Four Quadrants.[3] The two quadrants on the right point to the more familiar individual and collective exterior dimensions of experience, while the two on the left represent the often-underappreciated interior lives of individuals and collectives. To bring about holistic change, we need to engage all four.

If we merely concentrate on the external quadrants, we may find that even our best efforts to transform our lives and world can be undermined

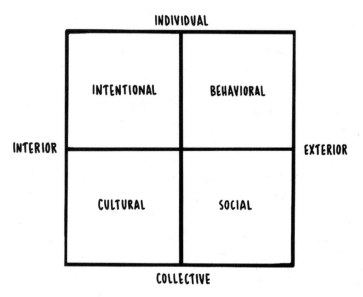

Figure 8.1: Ken Wilber's Four Quadrants.

by dysfunctional belief systems and patterns of behavior. On the other hand, inner work, by itself, isn't sufficient to bring about systems change.

Inner transformation is a necessary complement to engaging productively in external changemaking. Who we are determines what we think, what we think determines what we do, and what we do determines how we influence our world. Our capacity to help and heal the planet depends to a large extent on how well we have dealt with our fears and other ego-related fixations. If we can change ourselves, we can help others do the same.

While the definition of what the Inner Transition encompasses continues to be expanded and refined, many of its key pillars were established early on. Hopkins devoted nearly one-third of his *Transition Handbook* to exploring "How peak oil and climate change affect us," "Understanding the psychology of change," and "Harnessing the power of a positive vision." Sophy Banks similarly embedded a presentation on healing from trauma, a discussion about shifting belief systems, and multiple activities from Joanna Macy's Work That Reconnects into Transition Launch Training.

Of course, many other philosophies and practices could be incorporated into the Inner Transition, and innovation should continue to be welcomed in this area. However, it's my belief that it should always remain nonsectarian and focused exclusively on supporting people who are actively engaged in changemaking work. Although we can and should feel free to draw from a wide variety of authentic wisdom traditions, it's important we don't pigeonhole Transition by aligning too closely with any one. We should also definitely not be in the business of creating a new religion or offering the Inner Transition as a substitute for psychotherapy when needed.

This chapter will draw on the knowledge and experience I've gained through studying and practicing Tibetan Buddhism over the past two and a half decades. However, I want to be clear from the outset that I'm not trying to convert anyone. This simply happens to be the tradition I'm most familiar with. Many other traditions teach similar concepts and practices, and I'm counting on you to translate what I'm presenting into whatever language works for you. Ultimately, truth is truth wherever we find it, and reality is much bigger than any one sect. Religion should be used as a tool to promote human flourishing, not wielded as a weapon to divide us.

Paradigm Shift

Because our fundamental beliefs are the wellspring of everything we do, reflecting on them is a natural starting point for our explorations of the Inner Transition. If we think people are basically selfish and confused and that life is fundamentally pointless and chaotic, we're unlikely to even entertain the thought of working with others to try to improve conditions. However, if we believe life is a miracle, full of endless possibilities, there's no limit to what we might do to manifest the better world we envision.

The dominant culture of our times tends to approach life as a battle, humanity as suspect, and nature as either scenery to be ignored or a resource to be exploited, so we need to be on guard against these insidious ideas, which tend to promote cynicism, disconnection, and conflict. Fortunately, there are other cultures we can look to that instead emphasize the sacredness and interrelatedness of all existence, encouraging open-mindedness, empathy, and reciprocity.

The Shambhala tradition, of which I am a part, describes its central philosophy as one of "basic goodness," a term that's roughly synonymous with the more traditional Buddhist concept of "buddha nature." Basic goodness says that our highest potential is contained within our deepest self and that all sentient beings have the ability to access innate wisdom that is naturally compassionate. This doesn't mean we're always right no matter what we do or that everything is perfect just as it is. Our basic goodness may be partly or entirely obscured for a moment or a lifetime, but it never stops shining and cannot be destroyed.

While this might sound too good to be true, basic goodness has increasingly become my default state of being and everyday experience. Through many painful repetitions of trial and error, I've gradually come to accept that when I'm connected with my basic goodness, I'm happier and able to be of greater help to others. Contrary to my worst fears, letting go of my habitual distrust of myself and others didn't cause me to stop caring and trying to do my best. Instead, I found that I became more intuitive, patient, and creative. Insights and energies that had previously been tied up in inner conflict were freed to be used in more productive ways, and powerful synchronicities began to occur. What previously felt like a struggle has gradually become more and more effortless.

Not coincidentally, holding this perspective of basic goodness (or whatever we want to call it) supports a shift from conventional activism to evolutionary change. It makes us more holistic, motivated primarily by hope and possibility, unafraid to take action, and open to synergistic collaboration. This is how we embody the change we want to see in the world.

Nevertheless, this way of being can be difficult to accept. It offers us no guarantees or fixed reference points to fall back on. It forces us to think on our feet, often without a clear destination. It frequently steers us towards what we fear the most and away from the person we thought we were. As a result, it requires tremendous courage to stick with it in the face of a culture that tells us it's naive, delusional, and possibly even dangerous. In contrast, the predict-and-control mentality promoted by the Industrial Growth Society promises that if we only work hard enough and do what we're told, we'll be safe and comfortable, successful and respected.

Of course, this is a lie, but in pointing that out, I'm not implying we should automatically reject everything our culture teaches us. Even if that were possible, it wouldn't be wise. In situations of immediate threat, a shot of adrenaline can help us outrun the danger, and sometimes the best solution is simply to yank on the biggest lever we can find.

Basic goodness, in its deepest sense, transcends attachment to any particular paradigm. It's fundamentally the act of trusting our intuitive perception of what's being called for in any given situation. A traditional metaphor for this is dancing with reality. When you're dancing, if you have to even think about what to do next, you're already a step behind. Instead, you need to let go to be moved by the music. In the beginning, it's awkward, but over time, you know exactly what to do.

Practice and Path

As intriguing as basic goodness is as a philosophy, it isn't just another concept we can add to our concept collection. If we want to be fundamentally transformed by it and reap its many benefits, we have to learn to live into it, which can only be accomplished through sustained contemplation and practice.

While there are many valuable inner work practices we can choose from (including prayer, art, yoga, ceremony, journaling, psychotherapy, and spending time in nature), they aren't all the same. Each helps us cultivate some aspects of ourselves, but not others. Some are primarily contemplative, while others are mostly meditative or expressive.

Because we are complex, multifaceted beings, it can be beneficial to engage in more than one practice at a time. However, if we don't root ourselves in at least one, we may find ourselves endlessly skating on the surface without ever accessing the full depth of what they're able to provide. Although trying out different practices makes sense initially, we eventually need to commit.

My main practice has long been Shamatha-Vipashyana meditation. *Shamatha* is usually translated from the Sanskrit as "calm abiding," while *Vipashyana* is typically rendered as "insight." The basic idea is that, out of the stillness of Shamatha, Vipashyana insight naturally arises.

In the style of meditation I practice, one begins by assuming a posture that is both upright and relaxed, sitting cross-legged on a cushion on the floor or in a chair, and following the breath as it flows in and out. Whenever we notice we've become distracted by thoughts, we simply acknowledge that and gently bring our attention back to the present moment. By repeatedly letting go of our preoccupations and coming back to ourselves, we gradually develop peace, clarity, and inner freedom.

In scientific terms, what we are doing in meditation is training ourselves to spend less time in our sympathetic nervous system, caught up in fight, flight, freeze, and fawn reactivity, and more in our parasympathetic nervous system, with its capacity for equanimity, resilience, learning, and growth. Neuroplasticity means that, with sufficient practice, even our most entrenched patterns of thought and behavior can be altered.

When I started meditating regularly in college, my experience was nothing like the breezy, blissed-out images of meditators you see in glossy magazines. Instead, I found the practice to be more difficult, disturbing, and disorienting than anything else. It was as if the light of my awareness had been cranked up all the way, illuminating all of the dark corners of which I had previously been oblivious.

Nevertheless, for reasons I still don't completely understand, I stuck with it, and as the years passed, I began to experience real benefits. I found myself becoming happier, more grounded, and confident. Because I was no longer overwhelmed by my personal problems, I could extend myself further to others. Now, although my meditative journey is far from over, basic goodness has begun to pervade every aspect of my life.

In Tibetan Buddhism, this three-stage process is referred to as the journey of the Three Yanas.[4] It encompasses the narrow path of the Hinayana, the broader path of the Mahayana, and the ultimate path of the Vajrayana. As with all developmental models, we don't leave behind earlier stages as we progress. The traditional metaphor for this is a building that has a solid foundation, four walls (with doors and windows), and a golden roof.

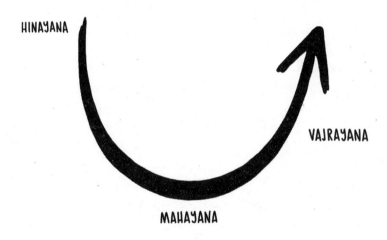

HINAYANA

VAJRAYANA

MAHAYANA

Figure 8.2: The Three Yanas, plotted against a U shape.

This logic is worth trying to understand. Before we can bring our vision into the wider world (Mahayana) and claim our full power as agents of regeneration (Vajrayana), we need to focus on ourselves (Hinayana). Towards the beginning of our journey, we are typically so confused that any attempt to exert greater influence over our world would be misguided. We have to get our own house in order, so to speak, before we can help others do the same.

The Hinayana teaches us how to work with our minds, develop self-discipline, and stop being a nuisance to our world. Once we've done that, we naturally find ourselves being drawn outward, onto the Mahayana path of the bodhisattva. The bodhisattva's full-time job is to free others from suffering and help them manifest their basic goodness. Bodhisattvas are often described as spiritual warriors, not because they are in any way aggressive but because they refuse to back down from any challenge.

The activities of a bodhisattva are called "the Six Paramitas" or six transcendent actions: generosity, patience, discipline, exertion, meditation, and wisdom.[5] Although these transcendent actions are primarily developed through meditation and the practice of everyday life, the Mahayana also offers specific techniques designed to increase selflessness and compassion such as Tonglen and the Four Immeasurables.

The Vajrayana is considered a fruitional stage. While the Hinayana and Mahayana are about improving ourselves and progressing on our path, the Vajrayana suggests our desire to get somewhere else or become a different person has now become our main obstacle. For this reason, Vajrayana practitioners typically spend a lot of time visualizing themselves as fully realized beings and their world as a sacred mandala, not to glorify their egos but to better connect with things as they actually are.

From just this brief description, you can probably understand why the details of the Vajrayana have historically been kept secret. Without thorough training in the Hinayana and Mahayana first, practitioners could easily misinterpret its message and try to manipulate its power. If we mistakenly believe we are already enlightened, anything we do can be justified, even if it harms others. Here as elsewhere, attempting to skip stages can be dangerous.

Discovering Purpose

Especially in these times, when our world is crying out for help in so many ways, it can be overwhelming to consider what we should be doing with our lives. Should I become a parent, helping to raise the next generation up right? Or a farmer, building local food security? Should I try to make the place where I already work better or drop everything to become a full-time activist? If I become an activist, should I try to save the rainforest or end police brutality? What would make the biggest impact?

As compelling as these questions are, I don't think asking ourselves What should I be doing? or How can I make the biggest impact? is the right way to approach discovering purpose. In this, I tend to agree with Howard Thurman, who said: "Don't ask yourself what the world needs. Ask yourself what makes you come alive, and go do that, because what the world needs is people who have come alive."[6] While this might sound like just a bunch of New Age mumbo-jumbo, it's worth considering that Thurman is best known for being a mentor to Dr. Martin Luther King Jr. and many other prominent leaders throughout the US civil rights movement.

I've found this to be true in my own life. When I'm engaged in work I'm deeply passionate about, I'm more inspired, more effective, and willing to go the extra mile. I've also noticed that, when I'm guided by my intrinsic sense of purpose, opportunities seem to present themselves as if by magic. As Joseph Campbell remarked in the PBS series *The Power of Myth*:

> If you do follow your bliss, you put yourself on a kind of track that has been there all the while, waiting for you, and the life that you ought to be living is the one you're living. Somehow, well, you can see it, and you begin to deal with people who are in the field of your bliss, and they open doors to you. I say follow your bliss and don't be afraid, and doors will open where you didn't know they were going to be.[7]

I know I happen to be one of the lucky ones. Most people feel so constrained by circumstances that they avoid asking themselves who they really want to be their entire lives. While this is understandable, it's ultimately self-defeating. Even if we're unable to realize our dreams right now, we can at least start taking steps in their general direction.

We might not feel like we know enough yet or have the right credentials. Nevertheless, we could begin by simply looking within, asking ourselves what we truly love, and suspending our judgment about what arises. Only after doing this should we turn to consider the more mundane questions of what we're good at, what our world needs, and what we can be paid for.

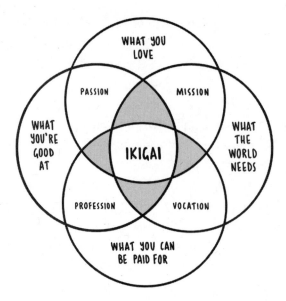

Figure 8.3: Ikigai.

These questions are connected with a Japanese concept called *Ikigai*, which translates as "a reason for being" and can help us uncover our own sense of purpose and direction. If you're willing, try sitting in silence in a place that deeply inspires you to calm and clear your mind. Then, draw the four intersecting circles depicted above on a piece of paper and ask yourself: what do I love, what am I good at, what does the world need, and what can I be paid for? Allow yourself plenty of time to consider each question and write down your responses before reflecting on how they might all be connected.

It's important to remember that we can't do everything that we want or is needed. If we try, we'll end up spreading ourselves too thin to make a real difference. Only by committing a significant portion of our time and energy to a focused pursuit over many years will we be able to make a meaningful and lasting impact.

Anything worth devoting our lives to is bound to be challenging. I've often thought that if people really understood how much work it would be to raise a child beforehand, a lot fewer would choose to become parents. Despite this, most parents speak of raising children as the most important and rewarding thing they've ever done.

The best-case scenario is that we may eventually come to experience our work as a true calling. In his *Letters to a Young Poet*, Rainer Maria Rilke writes:

> There is only one thing you should do. Go into yourself. Find out the reason that commands you to write; see whether it has spread its roots into the very depths of your heart; confess to yourself whether you would have to die if you were forbidden to write. This most of all: ask yourself in the most silent hour of your night: *must* I write? Dig into yourself for a deep answer. And if this answer rings out in assent, if you meet this solemn question with a strong, simple *"I must,"* then build your life in accordance with this necessity; your whole life, even into its humblest and most indifferent hour, must become a sign and witness to this impulse.[8]

From Burnout to Balance

Even if we're able to embrace our sense of purpose, that initial spark of inspiration can burn out over time if we're not careful. If we want to be able to follow our path all the way to its fruition, we must learn how to take good care of ourselves.

Although burnout is well-known as a potential pitfall throughout the activist community, many of us keep falling into it again and again. Depending on how you count it, I've burned out at least four times over the past two decades. However, each time I've learned more about why it happens. This has enabled me to bounce back more quickly and maybe even prevent burnout entirely by recognizing its early warning signs and knowing the right antidotes to apply.

Conventionally, burnout is understood simply as the result of working too hard for too long, and the remedy prescribed is the ubiquitous "self-care." While taking time off, exercising, eating healthy, and spending more time with friends undoubtedly helps, we should consider other reasons and strategies as well.

Simply trying to remain conscious in these times isn't easy. As tough as organic farming can be on the body, I've always found my work with the

Transition Movement to be even more exhausting. I believe this is because it's so intellectually demanding and emotionally charged. For this reason, when I was executive director of Transition US, I changed our definition of full-time work from 40 to 32 hours per week. Even that much time spent wrestling with humanity's biggest problems is probably unsustainable over the long run.

Burnout can also be caused by persistent feelings of disempowerment and hopelessness. If we lack agency in our current role or doubt that our efforts are really making a difference, we should take that as a sign to speak up or make a change. If we don't, we risk suppressing and internalizing our discontent. While we may be able to push through these feelings for a while, we eventually have to reckon with reality. When we can no longer tolerate our situation, we may already feel so drained and defeated that we may be inclined to give up altogether.

Working to make the world a better place is never going to be easy, but we can learn how to modulate our stress so it doesn't become debilitating. Although a certain amount of disequilibrium is necessary for growth, pushing ourselves beyond our limits for too long is counterproductive.

One framework I've found to be useful for navigating this territory is called the "Learning Zone Model." I first came across it when I worked

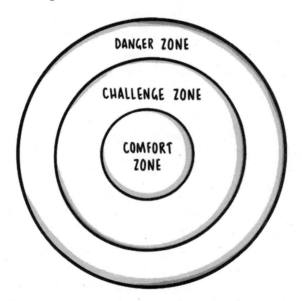

Figure 8.4: Learning Zones.

for Outward Bound and used to teach it to my teenage students. It's both incredibly simple and surprisingly profound.

As you can see, it consists of three concentric circles. The smallest circle in the center is our "Comfort Zone." Beyond that, we have a "Learning Zone" (which is sometimes called our "Challenge Zone") and a "Panic Zone" (or "Danger Zone"). The basic idea is to spend as much time as possible in our Challenge Zone without tipping ourselves over into danger. As we repeatedly stretch ourselves in this way, our Comfort Zone expands while our Danger Zone naturally contracts.

Sometimes these zones are color coded (green for Comfort, yellow for Challenge, and red for Danger) to make them even easier to remember. However, because the contents and dimensions of these zones vary from person to person and moment to moment, the only way we can really know where we are is by cultivating direct awareness of our state of being. If we can do that, we'll be able to intuitively sense when we need to rest and when we need to push forward.

When doing stressful work, we should check in with ourselves periodically and ask whether we're currently in the green, yellow, or red. When I've been running in the red too long, my favorite thing to do is take a nap. Often, I fall asleep, while other times, I simply lie down on my back with my eyes closed, tune into my breath, and imagine all of the stress in my body and mind gradually melting down into the Earth. Either way, I almost always rise up after a half an hour or so feeling refreshed. Playing music or going for a long walk tends to have a similar effect.

Another tool I've developed for preventing burnout is what I've come to call the Mandala of Life. It attempts to take the Mandala of the Five Buddha Families, which I described in chapter 2 as a pattern of Wholeness, and translate it into a guide for maintaining balance in everyday life. In this context, the Buddha Buddha family represents our physical and spiritual well-being, which needs to be firmly planted in the center. The Vajra Buddha family symbolizes our need to always be developing ourselves intellectually. The Ratna Buddha family is connected with home and community, the Padma Buddha family with love and self-expression, and the Karma Buddha family with service to our wider world.

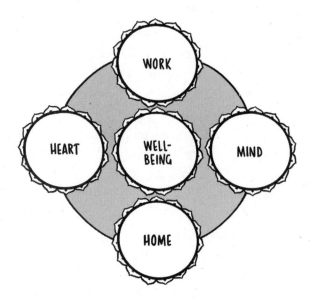

Figure 8.5: The Mandala of Life.

All five of these elements need to be continually attended to. I find that if I neglect any one for too long, I become wobbly, like a chair that's missing a leg.

I typically use the Mandala of Life simply by calling it to mind every so often and asking myself what I'm doing to nurture myself in each of these five areas. Then, I reflect on how well they're currently balanced and where I might need to pay more attention. Occasionally, I even draw these five circles on a piece of paper and take written notes.

Try creating your own mandala and asking yourself these same questions. However, in doing so, we shouldn't be trying to stuff ourselves into little boxes. After all, our life is more like an ever-changing river than a tidy to-do list. If we can embrace our basic goodness, embody it through practice, live into our deepest purpose, and maintain an ongoing sense of balance, the mandala of our life will unfold on its own.

We can really only help others when we are healthy and whole in ourselves. As our world becomes increasingly unstable, inner work will become even more essential. During the first few months of the pandemic, when many people were losing their minds and climbing the walls in isolation, I found that I could easily adjust to this new reality and pivot to what was needed because of the inner resilience I had developed over so many years. If we begin preparing ourselves now, we'll all be better off when the next crisis inevitably hits.

9

Healthy Groups

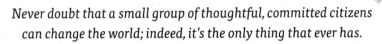

Never doubt that a small group of thoughtful, committed citizens
can change the world; indeed, it's the only thing that ever has.

— Margaret Mead[1]

Although regeneration begins with us as individuals, we eventually have to join with others for it to ripple out into the world. We need other people not only to share in the work but also to shed light on our blind spots and remind us we aren't alone.

Because nearly all social change originates within small groups, cultivating their effectiveness is of the utmost importance. If a group is adrift without a clear purpose, its members merely struggling to get along with each other and make decisions, the change this group will be able to affect in the world is likely to be minimal. However, if we can cultivate healthy and harmonious groups in which every member is able to fully contribute their knowledge, insights, skills, and creativity, our small groups can become incredibly powerful seedbeds of change.

Most of us have been thoroughly trained in how hierarchies function because our families, schools, workplaces, and governments are all organized this way. They're shaped like a pyramid with a boss at the top and everyone else sorted into levels of diminishing influence below. Power typically only flows in one direction. Subordinates are expected to do what they're told and report back to their superiors. Punishments and rewards are handed down from above.

While hierarchies do exist in nature (think of chickens with their infamous pecking order) and are sometimes appropriate and necessary (as in the relationship between a parent and child), they also have the potential to act as powerful forces of oppression. Even at their best, hierarchies tend to stifle creativity, breed disconnection and resentment, and rob organizations of their collective intelligence and vitality. For all of these reasons and more, an increasing number of groups are searching for other ways to structure themselves.

Alternatives to hierarchy are readily available, but most of us haven't been taught how to use them. As a result, groups trying to work in a collaborative way without putting in place processes and structures that facilitate collaboration usually find themselves bogged down in indecision and conflict, and often end up creating shadow hierarchies to get work done. Based on my observations, dysfunctional internal dynamics are, by far, the leading cause of activist groups falling apart.

I was already well aware of this problem when I traveled to Los Angeles in 2013 to train with Nick Osborne, a UK-based leader in nonhierarchical organizational development, who had recently created a course for Transition Network called Effective Groups. Although I had previously taken many other classes and workshops on similar topics, I found Nick's curriculum to be more accessible, practical, and comprehensive than any I had encountered. For this reason, I became an Effective Groups Trainer and continue to teach an updated version of this course.

Although there are quite a few differences between Effective Groups Training and what I present in this chapter, both are organized around the Stages of Group Development.[2]

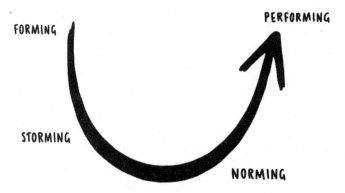

Figure 9.1: The Stages of Group Development, plotted against a U shape.

In brief, Forming is about putting in place the foundational elements necessary to support a group through the earliest stages of its development. This includes recruiting an initial leadership team, cultivating trusting relationships between members, establishing group agreements, and developing shared purpose. While we may be tempted to try to design everything perfectly from the outset, anticipating every potential scenario, this is impossible, unnecessary, and counterproductive. Instead, we should recognize that effective collaboration is always a work in progress that unfolds organically over time.

Forming is often experienced as a honeymoon stage, in which everyone is getting along reasonably well and there's a lot of excitement about the group's future possibilities. It's usually only once people feel settled and the real work begins that conflict starts to bubble up. While there's a tendency to interpret Storming as a sign of failure, it's actually an essential part of the overall progression. If we prepare ourselves adequately beforehand and lean into the storm when it comes, we will emerge stronger and wiser on the other side.

On the other side of Storming is Norming. Having been refined in the fire of challenge and conflict, we're now able to upgrade and expand the systems we established in Forming. For most groups, this involves fundraising to build capacity and becoming a larger and more impactful organization.

Developing a highly functional and sustainable organization in Norming opens the door to Performing. Of course, Performing isn't a static state. We frequently cycle back through earlier stages as circumstances change and members come and go. However, Performing isn't a myth either. We can actually learn how to collaborate effectively and eventually serve as a model for others.

Doing so requires that we periodically reflect on how our group is working together and make needed improvements. If we're always pushing forward with action, we'll end up neglecting our relationships with each other and missing out on important opportunities to learn from experience. Conversely, if we spend all our time looking inward, we won't generate enough momentum to keep members engaged. Although the right balance between action and reflection fluctuates from stage to stage and group to group, we always need to make time for both.

Forming

Prior to launching a new group, we should take whatever time is needed to really get to know the community we're intending to serve and find out what similar work is underway first. Starting a new initiative from scratch is a massive undertaking, and we don't want to compete with related groups for attention and resources. If one close enough to what you're envisioning already exists, you might consider simply joining that group and helping to strengthen it.

The Initiating Group: If after doing your due diligence, however, you decide to start a new group, it pays to be thoughtful about how you do that. Instead of putting out a general call to anyone who wants to join your Initiating Group, you might consider finding out who's interested first, then sitting down with them to discuss whether or not they'd be a good fit. It's generally much easier to start with a small committed team and expand it later than begin with one that's much too large and unwieldy. I usually find five to eight members to be ideal for new groups.

What I look for first when recruiting new group members is that they already care deeply about the issues we'll be working together to address. I've occasionally referred to this as "having Transition in the heart." It's my number one criteria because I want to make sure everyone's getting involved for the right reasons, not because they want to push some hidden agenda. This also tells me they're likely to work hard and aren't just signing on to pad their resume. After that, I tend to look for people who are responsible, even-tempered, strategic thinkers that generally get along well with everyone.

While these qualities promote unity in groups, diversity is equally important. Ecosystems thrive because they include many different species interacting symbiotically. In addition to recruiting people from diverse backgrounds, we should also seek to include at least three different types of members: Charismatic Visionaries, Skilled Specialists, and Community Connectors.

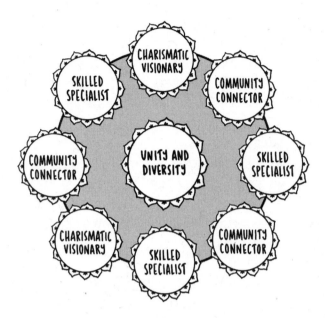

Figure 9.2: Initiating Group structure.

With their talent for dreaming big and inspiring others, Charismatic Visionaries are obviously important. However, the other two types are no less so. Skilled Specialists may be accountants, fundraisers, farmers, lawyers, engineers, event planners, or computer programmers who provide needed expertise. Community Connectors are social butterflies who tend to know people everywhere they go and are willing to draw on their connections to help our cause.

Although some people embody more than one type, most have a dominant characteristic. The basic idea is that your more pragmatic members balance and complement those who are more idealistic (and vice versa). When forming a group, we may have to proceed with a coalition of the willing, but over time, we can fill in the gaps.

Group Agreements: Once our Initiating Group has formed, we should allow plenty of time for members to get to know each other and figure out how they'll work best together. While group agreements may not seem necessary when everything's going great, when there's disagreement, they give us something to fall back on. The process of forming group agreements also helps make implicit assumptions explicit and clarifies the rules of the game. Although we might assume we're all on the same page already, we may actually have very different ideas about what constitutes acceptable behavior, how we should communicate with each other, and what the basic responsibilities of group members should be.[3]

To offer an analogy, I was playing gin rummy with a couple of friends a few years ago when we suddenly realized we were playing by different sets of rules. I had grown up playing it one way, and each of my friends had learned it differently. If we had discussed this at the outset, we could have decided which rules to follow. However, now that points were at stake, things got a bit heated. In this case, we were able to resolve our conflict before it got out of hand, but I can imagine if we were back in the Wild West and enough money was on the line, there might have been a shootout.

The process of creating group agreements is fairly simple. It usually begins with a facilitator inviting members to suggest agreements they would like to see adopted. To get the ball rolling, the facilitator might suggest a few common examples, such as not interrupting each other, making decisions by consensus, and ensuring equal airtime for all members. Then, after an initial brainstorm, the facilitator guides the group back through each proposed agreement, encouraging questions, objections, and revisions before voting to approve them or not. Approved agreements should be carefully recorded, shared with all members, and updated whenever new ones are made.

Shared Purpose: Once we have some basic group agreements in place, they can support the development of shared purpose. The process for developing shared purpose I learned from Nick tends to work well in my experience. It starts with developing a shared vision, then using that to create a mission and goals.

For developing shared vision, you could use the Visioning a Post-Transition World exercise I described in chapter 7. As previously mentioned, your vision should attempt to be as inclusive, realistic, and inspiring as possible. Here's the vision statement I wrote for Transition Sarasota:

IMAGINE...living in a community that is walkable, bikeable, and busable. One where your food is healthy, fresh from a local farm or straight from your own garden. Where all voices are heard and people look after each other. Where there is a network of local businesses that can thrive in any economy. Where our energy comes from clean, renewable sources. Where people are united by a common purpose and nature is protected to be enjoyed by all. This is the vision of Transition Sarasota. Together, we can work to make it a reality.

While vision statements present what a group hopes to ultimately accomplish, mission statements define what it actually does. A group's mission can be thought of as its North Star, a fixed point that shines the brightest out of a universe of infinite possibilities. As such, we can use it to navigate by, not just in times of smooth sailing, but especially in rougher seas. In just a few sentences, your mission statement should clearly explain to readers what your initiative is all about.

When I wrote an initial mission statement for Transition Sarasota, I framed our group's purpose this way:

The mission of Transition Sarasota is to act as a catalyst for rebuilding local community resilience and self-reliance in response to the converging crises of fossil fuel depletion, climate change, and economic instability. Through educational programs and innovative projects, Transition Sarasota seeks to revitalize local agriculture, strengthen our local economy, reduce our dependence on fossil fuels, and serve as an inspiration and model for other communities who wish to do the same.

However, as Transition Sarasota has been forced to scale back somewhat in recent years, our mission has likewise been pared back to "We create food and economic security by supporting local, sustainable sources." Even if your group's vision remains the same, its mission may change over time in response to changing circumstances.

You might create your group's mission statement by brainstorming key concepts, then clustering similar concepts and deciding which are most important to include. Instead of attempting to wordsmith your statement on the spot, which can be extremely tedious, you might invite everyone to write their own statement, discuss the parts you like the best, and combine them into a final version.

Your goals will change even more frequently than your mission and should be revised at least once a year. For goals to be as useful as possible, they should be SMART (Specific, Measurable, Assigned, Realistic, and Timed).[4] Goals should be Specific, so everyone knows what's been agreed to; they should be Measurable, so we can determine whether we've met them or not; and they should be Assigned, because if no one commits to carry out an action, it usually doesn't happen. They should also be Realistic, aligned with current capacity, and Timed, so they don't just drag on indefinitely.

SMART goals give us targets to shoot for and ways of measuring progress. However, this doesn't mean that we won't occasionally miss our targets, especially if we've set them too high or too close. While goals should stretch us, they should also be within our power to achieve. Continually falling short of our stated intentions can be demoralizing, so it's generally better to set modest goals at first and gradually scale up our ambitions over time.

Storming

At some point, the honeymoon always has to end. However, if we've adequately prepared ourselves in Forming, we can weather the coming storm and even turn it to our advantage. To do this, we need to stop trying to suppress conflict and embrace it as an opportunity to accelerate our development. As we all know, ignoring and avoiding conflict doesn't make it go away. Instead, it festers beneath the surface, corroding relationships and piling up resentments until they explode. For this reason, it's generally easier to deal with conflicts as they arise, while they're still relatively small and manageable.

Conflict Resolution Policy: To manage conflict successfully, it first needs to be held in a sturdy container. Otherwise, it can easily spiral out of control or resurface repeatedly without ever being resolved. Establishing a conflict resolution policy that all group members explicitly commit to can provide the necessary container for conflicts to be processed productively.

In talking about conflict, I'm not just referring to spectacular blowups where people are at each other's throats. More often, conflict manifests as a persistent sense of injustice or frustration about how our group is operating. One common source of conflict is members failing to abide by agreements they previously made. Looked at in this way, the following process can also be understood as a tool for us to hold each other accountable to our commitments.

The process I recommend comes from the Boulder Housing Coalition, which runs four co-op houses, including the one where I currently live. It starts by encouraging those who are directly involved in the conflict to try to resolve their issues among themselves first if possible. However, if emotions are running high in the moment, all parties are entitled to take a break to cool down before reconvening. Depending on your context, you might want to limit this cool-down period to a few days or a couple of weeks.

If the parties directly involved in the conflict aren't able to resolve it among themselves, they're then invited to ask for help. By the time the conflict has surfaced, trust and communication may have already broken down to the extent that some form of mediation is needed. This can be provided by another group member who has the necessary skills and is perceived as neutral by everyone, or someone can be brought in from outside. Professional mediators can usually be found nearby through a simple internet search.

If the conflict still isn't resolved through mediation, it's brought to the group as a whole. At this point, those not directly involved in the conflict have the authority to decide what conditions must be met for all parties to remain in good standing. If these conditions aren't met or the conflict is deemed irreconcilable, the group then has the right to ask members to leave. While expulsion should only be used as a last resort, if a member has proven an unwillingness to resolve conflicts or consistently uphold group agreements, this may be necessary to preserve the health of the whole.

Ideally, this process or a similar one would be established before conflict erupts. In the heat of the moment, having to decide how conflict will be processed makes it even more difficult to address. It's always a good idea to have your conflict resolution policy written down, so it can be referred to later, and require every new member to sign it before joining.

Conflict Transformation Process: As important as it is to establish a conflict resolution policy, this merely provides the container in which conflict can be safely held. Equally important is how we communicate with each other inside that container. The most helpful methodology I've found for this is Nonviolent Communication (NVC).

Originally developed in the 1960s by Marshall Rosenberg, NVC has been used to resolve conflicts as serious as sexual abuse and civil war, but is more commonly used to address minor disagreements and improve everyday communication. NVC has gotten a bad rep in some circles because people sometimes use it in manipulative ways. However, it's meant to foster compassion towards those we are engaged in conflict with and generate solutions that benefit everyone. When some use it to invalidate the communication styles of others or insist that they speak according to an unfamiliar set of rules, they are acting against the true spirit of NVC.

Because NVC is a vast subject, I'm choosing to focus specifically on its Four Steps. If you want to go deeper, there are many excellent resources available through the Center for Nonviolent Communication.[5]

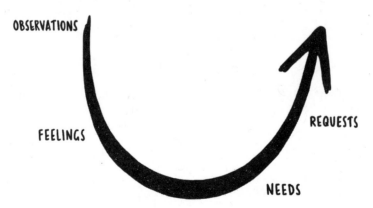

OBSERVATIONS

FEELINGS

NEEDS

REQUESTS

Figure 9.3: The Four Steps of Nonviolent Communication, plotted against a U shape.

The first step in the NVC process is exchanging our Observations about the conflict, without judgment, with each other. While this is partly about establishing facts, it's also crucial to recognize that different people may honestly perceive the same situation differently. Instead of stubbornly clinging to our own version of events, we're encouraged to try to understand other perspectives. By doing so, we develop a more complete picture of the conflict.

The purpose of the second step, Feelings, is to communicate how this conflict has directly impacted us. Here again, we are attempting to separate our ideas about what happened from what actually occurred. By vulnerably sharing our Feelings with each other, we deepen mutual understanding and open a door to genuine empathy.

The third step of the NVC process is about reflecting on what unmet Needs may have triggered these Feelings. At this point, we're encouraged to dig beneath the surface to identify root causes. We all have fundamental human needs and suffer when they aren't met. While we're not responsible for meeting anyone else's needs (and others aren't responsible for meeting ours), understanding the needs underlying conflict provides a basis for figuring out how to transform it.

The final step is to exchange Requests. However, this isn't just about asking for what we want. It's about seeking a solution that actually resolves the root causes of the conflict and benefits everyone involved. As with the SMART goals I mentioned in the previous section, Requests should be Specific, Measurable, Assigned, Realistic, and Timed. Although they don't have to be granted, if you're unable to fulfill someone else's request, it's important to explain why and be willing to negotiate an alternative.

While it's useful to practice these Four Steps in a linear way at first, our goal should be to seamlessly integrate the principles of NVC into how we naturally speak. To become fluent in NVC, we need to suspend our assumptions, accept critical feedback, take ownership for our mistakes, and be willing to change. As such, I find it to be even more of an inner practice than an external technique. If we don't fundamentally transform ourselves, it doesn't matter how good our methodology is. We can always distort and misuse it.

Norming

By the time we've reached Norming, it's likely that our group has very different needs from those it had originally. While it's perfectly fine to start as an informal, all-volunteer group with no funding, initiatives that stay that way limit their ability to affect change in the world and tend not to last. Breaking through to a higher level of impact almost always requires becoming a formal organization and raising funds to support it.

Becoming a Formal Organization: In his Twelve Steps of Transition, Rob Hopkins suggested the first step Transitioners should take is to "Set up a steering group and design its demise from the outset." Although the term "steering group" has since been replaced by "Initiating Group" and "design its demise" has been changed to "design its evolution," Hopkins' main point remains valid. As a Transition Initiative grows and evolves, those who helped start the group may not be the best people to guide it later on. Recognizing this helps to counteract the tendency for group members to hold onto positions of power long after their leadership has become a liability, a condition commonly known as founder's syndrome.

One way we've already discussed that an Initiating Group can scale up is by catalyzing Working Groups around various themes. These Working Groups produce their own projects and events, and once enough of them have formed, the Initiating Group morphs into a larger Core Group that includes representatives from each Working Group. The Core Group then serves primarily to facilitate communication and cooperation throughout the initiative as a whole while allowing Working Groups a high degree of autonomy to organize themselves however they see fit.

Although this is a brilliant and effective strategy for enabling volunteers to step into leadership roles, it ignores the reality that most groups eventually incorporate as formal nonprofit organizations. This makes it possible for them to fundraise legally, exempts donations from being taxed, and confers some degree of mainstream respectability. It's also not nearly as difficult as most people think, at least here in the US. A small group of us filled out Transition Sarasota's application for federal 501(c)(3) status over lunch and were approved within a few months.[6]

If you're not ready yet to incorporate on your own, you might seek out a fiscal sponsor, but either way, the basic structure required of nonprofit organizations is the same. There's a Board of Directors that hires and supervises an Executive Director, who hires and supervises other Staff. At a minimum, the Board has a legal obligation to ensure Staff are carrying out the organization's stated mission, managing its finances responsibly, and abiding by all relevant legal and ethical guidelines. Staff work together to carry out strategy approved by the Board on a day-to-day basis.

Blending the structure of a Core Group (with representatives from various Working Groups) with that of a nonprofit organization (that has a Board of Directors and Staff) might look something like this:

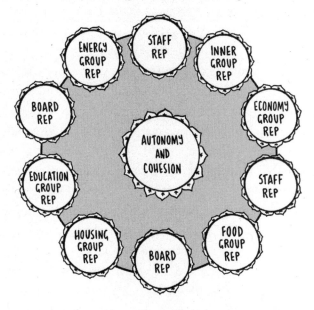

Figure 9.4: Core Group structure.

In this configuration, Staff are responsible for supporting Working Groups and ensuring their success. They might offer training in effective collaboration, work with groups to fundraise for their projects and events, help resolve conflicts, and provide leaders with access to personalized coaching and mentoring. Staff should also take the lead on establishing clear agreements between the organization as a whole and each Working Group.

These agreements might include the scope and mission of each Working Group, information about how the group will be governed, commitment to a set of core principles, what powers and authorities are being delegated from the organization to the Working Group, and what responsibilities each is expected to uphold. Having representatives from your Board of Directors in your Core Group is always a good idea to ensure they understand and prioritize the needs of those actually doing the work.

Fundraising: Many nonprofits run on a shoestring, but some funding is almost always required to sustain them. In addition to raising money for specific projects and events, we also need to fund coordination of the initiative as a whole. Otherwise, we may not be able to find anyone to do all of the tedious administrative work that's necessary to hold everything together. Hopkins has referred to this as "the doughnut effect," where "all the energy goes into emergent projects and enterprises while the core—which links everything together—goes empty. Providing income for paid staff for core activities can open up incredible opportunities."[7]

Cultivating a diverse mix of income streams can help an organization avoid becoming overly reliant on any one source, bolstering financial resilience. There are four main types of revenue for nonprofits: earned income, donations, sponsorships, and grants.

The easiest way to start raising funds is by charging modest registration fees or asking for suggested donations at workshops, trainings, and events. While it's always important to provide scholarships and other financial assistance for those who need it, many people are happy to contribute to a good cause. Beyond charging for events, we might also consider creating at least some of our practical projects as social enterprises that regularly feed a percentage of their profits back to the initiative as a whole.

To inspire individuals to donate to our organization, we first need to demonstrate that we're capable of making a meaningful impact and will put their contributions to good use. However, once we've done that, we shouldn't be shy about asking for money. If we truly believe in what we're doing, we should be eager to invite our community to support it. We might begin by organizing an annual fundraising party or emailing a series of heartfelt appeals to our mailing list around the holidays. Later, we might run online crowdfunding campaigns for specific projects and launch a general membership program with various levels and benefits.

Once we've established credibility and built a sizable following, we can start soliciting sponsorships. Because sponsorships are basically an exchange of money for exposure and recognition, we need to be careful about who we associate ourselves with. If we appear to be endorsing companies whose values don't align with our own, we may be complicit in greenwashing their reputation. Nevertheless, if we think about it, there are many different kinds of local businesses (such as solar installers, farm-to-table restaurants, farmers' markets, yoga studios, bike shops, and coffee shops) we might actually be proud to promote.

Grants tend to make up the lion's share of most nonprofit budgets. However, if we become too dependent on them, we may end up chasing after priorities that are not our own. Although most grants focus on specific time-limited projects that require detailed plans and clear deliverables, others support general operations. Government grants are typically harder to get and have even more rigorous reporting requirements than private foundations. As with individuals and business owners, cultivating personal relationships with grantmakers can greatly increase the chances they will fund your work.

I know many Transitioners who are hesitant to engage with these issues of money and power, and would prefer to stay small rather than risk getting bogged down in bureaucracy or corrupted by cash. Nevertheless, in this Great Transition, we need to recognize we are David facing Goliath. We can't possibly hope to counter the negative influence of national governments and multinational corporations with just a handful of volunteers. While the answer is obviously not to imitate the tactics of the Industrial Growth Society, we need to build power to achieve regeneration.

After all, a big part of what we're trying to do is give birth to a new economy. Why is it okay for some people to get paid handsomely for destroying the planet but not for others to earn a decent living helping to heal it? Not everyone can afford to volunteer. As Doria Robinson, executive director of Urban Tilth, said to Hopkins on stage at the 2013 Northern California Permaculture Convergence: "If this is a revolution that depends on volunteering, I can't be part of your revolution."[8] This is true for many people, especially those from disadvantaged frontline communities.

Performing

By engaging in the work of Forming, Storming, and Norming, we create many of the conditions necessary for collective intelligence to flourish in Performing. Our best-case scenario is that we eventually learn to function like a single organism whose whole is much greater than the sum of its parts. However, the old adage, "A camel is a horse designed by committee," points out that the opposite is also a possibility. Beyond what we've already discussed in this chapter, three additional factors are essential for achieving and maintaining high performance in groups: authentic collaboration, blended decision-making, and continuous learning.

Authentic Collaboration: For a group to develop collective intelligence, all of its members need to be fully engaged and contributing. Brian Robertson, the founder of Holacracy, tells a powerful story about this.[9] When he was first learning how to fly a plane, a warning light appeared on his dashboard that he didn't recognize. Observing that all of his other instruments were displaying normally, he chose to ignore it and nearly crashed as a result. Robertson's metaphor is that each member of our group acts like a sensor, picking up on different kinds of information, all of which are important for the group as a whole to pay attention to. As individuals, we have our biases and blind spots, but as a group, we can comprehend the panorama.

A few years ago, when we were developing an online version of Transition Thrive Training, my friend and fellow Transition Trainer Rebecca Blanco stumbled upon a model that can help us with this. The Thomas-Killman Conflict Modes describe five ways people typically interact in groups.

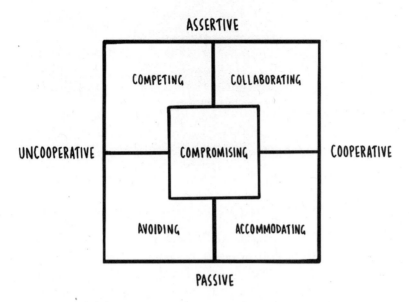

Figure 9.5: Thomas-Killman Conflict Modes.

While Accommodation and Avoidance manifest quite differently, they're actually two sides of the same coin. Avoidance is more obviously problematic, but too much Accommodation also signals an unwillingness to participate fully. If members aren't frequently expressing their opinions and volunteering for tasks, we should make an effort to reach out and ask why. There may be issues underneath the surface they don't feel comfortable discussing with the group.

Competition among group members can have many causes, but it's often a sign that people are feeling unheard or underappreciated. Because they believe they need to fight for respect and recognition, they act out and try to dominate conversations. This can be counteracted by ensuring that all group processes are inclusive, that group agreements are enforced fairly and consistently, and that all members are regularly celebrated for their contributions.

Compromise is, of course, sometimes necessary, but it becomes a problem when groups automatically default to it, habitually settling for the lowest common denominator. In Compromise, everybody typically gets some of what they want, but nobody is thrilled by the result.

Authentic Collaboration, on the other hand, eschews these kinds of trade-offs and seeks to weave only our best ideas together into a coherent and inspiring whole. Collaboration requires everyone to advocate passionately for what they believe in while also being willing to let go of attachment to any particular idea. Although what emerges from Collaboration may end up looking unlike anything anyone initially proposed, the outcome is usually more satisfying.

Blended Decision-Making: Consensus decision-making is a practical embodiment of the spirit of Collaboration. Because Consensus encourages everyone's participation and requires everybody's assent, it's the decision-making strategy most commonly adopted by activist groups. Never-

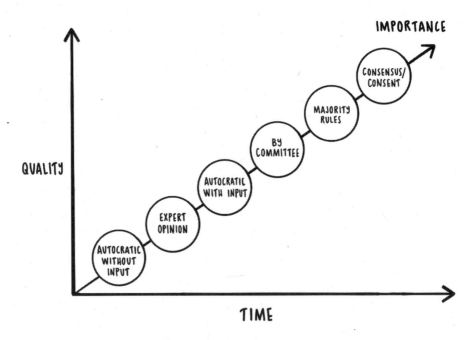

Figure 9.6: Blended decision-making.

theless, as many of us know all too well, Consensus often takes a lot longer than other processes and is sometimes impossible to achieve.

When we don't have the time Consensus demands, it can be appropriate to utilize other options. Before I took Nick Osborne's Effective Groups Training, I assumed groups had to pick one decision-making strategy and stick with it for every decision. Not only did I learn this isn't necessary, it's also hugely impractical. Even if a group has committed to using Consensus, it almost always delegates at least some decisions to individuals and subgroups, and employs alternative methods to overcome impasses. Nick refers to this as "blended decision-making."

While every decision-making strategy has its advantages and disadvantages, blended-decision-making can help us evaluate which strategies are most appropriate for which kinds of decisions.

Decision-making strategies that take the most time tend to produce the highest-quality results and should be used to guide our most complex, weighty, and far-reaching decisions. However, some decisions are fairly straightforward and less consequential. They might be delegated or voted on instead.

The worst thing we can do is say we're using Consensus when we actually aren't. I've observed groups whose idea of Consensus is somebody saying "This is what I want to do. How does everybody feel about that?" A couple of people nod or grunt incomprehensibly. Then, following a brief pause, the proposer announces: "Well, it's decided! We have consensus!" This is deeply problematic. Not only does it not provide any of the benefits Consensus is designed to deliver, it can also have the effect of alienating group members who feel understandably gaslit.

When you have a lot of important decisions to make, but not enough time to use Consensus for all of them, the next best alternative is the Consent process taught by Sociocracy.[10] These two processes are similar, but where Consensus aims for robust agreement, Consent settles for a lack of objections, using the standard of "good enough for now and safe enough to try." Because Consent tends to be quicker, decisions are more easily revised, enabling what's called "agile governance" and "dynamic steering."

Continual Learning: One final step we need to take to "unleash the collective genius" of our groups and organizations is to never stop learning and growing. Following a pattern that should be very familiar to you now, the Experiential Learning Cycle[11] suggests that instead of doing the same thing over and over and expecting different results, we can use every experience as an opportunity to experiment and innovate. Whatever we do, we should carefully observe both process and result, collect and analyze feedback, reflect on ways to improve in the future, and integrate lessons learned.

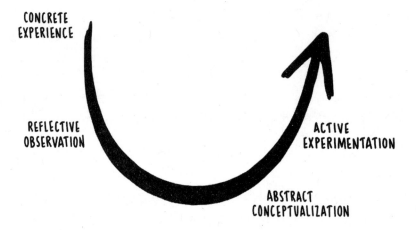

Figure 9.7: The Experiential Learning Cycle, plotted against a U shape.

As I mentioned in chapter 5, Transition Sarasota's first *Five Films for a Future* series was a big hit. However, when we launched our second series the following year, attendance began to drop. Although my first instinct was to blame people for not showing up, I chose to ask them instead why they weren't. By listening with an open mind, I came to understand that most were simply tired of watching documentaries and were ready to move on into action. As a result, Transition Sarasota subsequently pivoted towards more practical projects, and by doing so, continued to thrive.

In addition to direct observation and informally soliciting feedback, we should also regularly conduct formal assessments, both internally and externally, to measure progress towards our goals and identify strengths and weaknesses. Annual surveys and feedback forms distributed to participants following events are classic forms of external assessment. Examples of internal assessments include 360-degree performance reviews, in which everyone gives feedback to everyone else, and the Transition Healthcheck, which guides members through a process of evaluating the group as a whole.[12] Whatever methods you choose, what's most important is that information leads to action. Otherwise, it's just a waste of time.

Community Engagement

It really boils down to this: that all life is interrelated.
We are all caught in an inescapable network of mutuality,
tied into a single garment of destiny.
Whatever affects one directly, affects all indirectly.

—Dr. Martin Luther King Jr.[1]

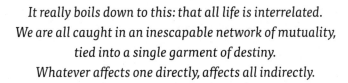

Community engagement is about building a movement big enough to matter, reaching beyond the small circle of our group to involve more and more people and partners over time. Ultimately, it's not enough to engage only those who already think the same way we do. We'll eventually need to find ways to inspire the apathetic, persuade the skeptical, and even convert some who currently see us as enemies into allies.

Fortunately, we don't have to win over everyone at once. Diffusion of Innovations Theory suggests that movement-building is inevitably a gradual process of Expansion that unfolds in five distinct waves. By first gaining the support of Innovators and Early Adopters, we can more easily persuade the Early Majority. Then, as more and more members of the Early Majority come onboard, that can lead to a tipping point, sweeping the Late Majority and maybe even some Laggards along as well.

Innovators are those who live on the leading edge. They are the people most likely to start new initiatives and step into leadership roles. All movements need Innovators to get the ball rolling, but they tend to be a fairly small group. According to Everett Rogers, whose 1962 book *Diffusion of Innovations* synthesized more than 500 studies,[2] Innovators typically only

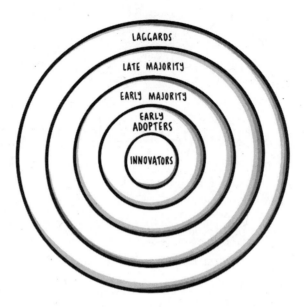

Figure 10.1: Diffusion of Innovations Theory, envisioned as a ripple pattern.

make up about 2.5 percent of a given population. Rogers estimated that Early Adopters represent around 13.5 percent; the Early and Late Majorities, 34 percent each; and Laggards, the remaining 16 percent.

While Early Adopters may not be the first to take the lead, their role as "first followers" is essential.[3] By their mere presence, they signal something important is happening. The genuine enthusiasm of Early Adopters also makes them good messengers and likely volunteers and donors. In political terms, they're our base.

In my experience, the Early Majority is full of well-meaning compassionate people who are sympathetic to our cause, at least in theory. They try to do the right thing in their personal lives, but don't feel they have the time, energy, or inclination to engage in activism. Nevertheless, if they can see our approach is working and gaining momentum, they might be persuaded to jump on board. Winning over the Early Majority is key to mainstreaming any movement.

Those in the Late Majority tend not to care about much beyond their own personal interests, but they are a large block, and if they see enough people heading in the same general direction, that will at least catch their attention. Although we may eventually win over some Laggards as well, I would caution against spending too much time trying to convince them, as many of these folks will probably never come around. That's fine. If we can get enough Innovators, Early Adopters, and members of the Early Majority onboard, that should be sufficient.

Harvard University political scientist Erica Chenoweth has made a case that a tipping point exists at 3.5 percent of a given population, but that number specifically refers to how many people need to be in the streets to force political concessions.[4] The best estimate I've seen for a cultural tipping point comes from a paper by researchers from the Universities of Pennsylvania and London.[5] Based on a series of psychological experiments, they concluded this number is probably closer to 25 percent. This suggests we may find ourselves at a tipping point as soon as we have won over about half of the Early Majority.

Raising Awareness

The Stages of Change described by Carlo DiClemente in his book *Addiction and Change*[6] have long been used to teach Transition leaders how to design a holistic program of awareness-raising events and other activities that maximizes community engagement. While it might seem strange to apply a model from addiction recovery to community organizing, the dynamics underlying how people change are essentially the same across different fields and scales.

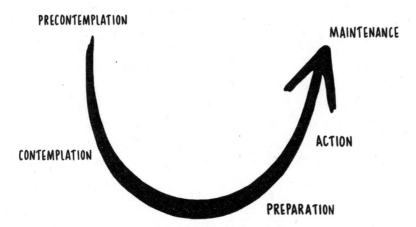

Figure 10.2: The Stages of Change, plotted against a U shape.

Precontemplation: At this stage, people haven't yet recognized or acknowledged there's a problem, so they're likely unaware our initiative even exists. While every group needs basic communications infrastructure such as a newsletter and website, we also have to find ways to break through the noise and meet people where they're at.

Although many activists continue to use social media as one of their main outreach strategies, I find its usefulness to be limited. In addition to artificially restricting the reach of posts that aren't paid for, social media algorithms tend to prioritize superficial, sensationalistic content and keep people segregated within homogenous filter bubbles.

At least on the local level, I've found mass media to be a much more effective strategy for breaking through to a larger and more diverse audience. One TV interview or article in the local paper can reach tens of thousands of people. Mainstream media attention, for better and worse, still signals to many people what's worth paying attention to and what's not. While we need to have a story worth telling, getting media coverage isn't as difficult as most people think, especially if the press releases we send out are able to connect whatever we're doing to topics of current interest. Once we've received coverage, it's easier to get more as we become more widely known throughout the community and cultivate personal relationships with journalists.

We also shouldn't underestimate the power of connecting in person. Although it's unlikely that those in the Precontemplation stage will show up at our events, we can go to them. Two of the most common ways change-making groups do this are by offering to give talks for other local organizations at their meetings and conferences, and tabling at community festivals and farmers' markets. However, you don't need to deliver a sterile Power-Point or have a boring informational booth with just a signup sheet for your mailing list and a pile of brochures. You could ask people to write or draw their own visions of the future, hand out free packets of seeds, or set up your own mini-bookstore with titles related to your work. Creativity like this is always encouraged.

Contemplation: At this stage, people are aware there's a problem but aren't sure yet if they actually want to do anything about it. These are the people we are trying to reach by offering awareness-raising events. I've found screening documentary films to be one of the easiest, most accessible, and engaging ways to rally people together and offer educational content. Other common awareness-raising strategies are to organize orientation meetings, book clubs, or a guest speaker series.

Regardless of the type of event, we should always design our awareness-raising events to allow plenty of time for attendees to meet and socialize, process the information that has been presented, and translate ideas into action. Incorporating food and art into events can also help them feel more alive.

The World Cafe is an especially effective format for facilitating Contemplation. Originally developed by Juanita Brown and David Issacs, it aims to create an atmosphere of casual intimacy that enables participants to relax and open up to each other. It does this by seating everyone around small cafe tables in groups of three to five. Often, World Cafe venues are beautifully decorated and every table is covered with a large sheet of paper and multicolored markers for anyone who wants to take notes or doodle as they talk.

Typically, there are three rounds of discussion exploring the same overarching theme, progressing from initial reflections to deeper analysis to practical applications. After each round, everyone except for the table host switches tables to build community and cross-pollinate ideas. Once all three rounds are complete, table hosts report key takeaways to the larger group.[7]

Preparation: People in this stage have decided to take action but are still figuring out what to do and how to do it. For them, we should provide training in both the hard and soft skills of regeneration. In the Transition Movement, training in the hard skills of growing, building, making, and fixing is referred to as the Great Reskilling, while instruction in the soft skills of community leadership and group facilitation usually comes under the banner of Transition Training.

Like World Cafe, Open Space Technology is a method of facilitating community conversations by breaking people into smaller groups. However, instead of providing the questions for each group to discuss, Open Space invites participants to propose and host concurrent sessions on topics of their own choosing. While a complete description of how Open Space works is beyond the scope of this book, "A Brief User's Guide to Open Space Technology" by its creator, Harrison Owen, can be downloaded online for free.[8]

Maintenance: The next chapter will be entirely focused on the Action stage, so I won't go into that here, but we shouldn't underestimate the importance of ongoing Maintenance. Creating spaces specifically for deepening our relationships with each other, reflecting and recharging, and acknowledging and celebrating both individual contributions and collective accomplishments can help people stay enthusiastically involved without burning out.

Because there will always be people at each of these stages, we should try our best to offer at least a little something for everyone. While we might not have the capacity to organize all five types of activities every month, we might be able to do that every few months or once a year. Otherwise, we'll fail to engage and retain a lot of good people who can't find anything that specifically addresses the stage they're in.

Of course, the Stages of Change are not the only dimension of difference we need to account for when planning a program of activities. We also need to design for those who have different interests and life circumstances. For example, some people will be drawn more to a workshop on bicycle repair than a presentation about climate science, and if we're holding an event on a weekday morning or afternoon, those who work 9 to 5 won't be able to come.

Partnerships and Coalitions

So far, we've been mostly looking at how to engage individuals, but engaging other organizations and institutions is at least as important. As with individuals, in the beginning, it's generally easier to partner with those who are already sympathetic to our cause (Innovators and Early Adopters). Then, once we've established a reputation for doing high-quality, impactful work, we'll have a better chance of convincing more mainstream groups (the Early and Late Majorities) to jump on board as well.

Tina Clarke, a fellow Transition Trainer, has developed an exercise called "The Big List"[9] that draws on Diffusion of Innovations Theory to teach community organizers how to develop a partnership strategy. In recent years, it has been taught alongside the Stages of Change as part of Transition Launch Training.

The first step in making a Big List is simply to brainstorm all of the groups that currently exist in your community that you might want to partner with in the future. These groups might include other nonprofits, cultural institutions, media outlets, sustainable businesses, foundations, government agencies, and key stakeholder groups. After just 10 to 15 minutes of brainstorming, most groups already have dozens of potential partners on their list.

The next step is to sort these potential partners into categories according to whether you consider them to be Ones (Innovators), Twos (Early Adopters), Threes (Early Majority), Fours (Late Majority), or Fives (Laggards). For groups that are just starting out, Tina suggests primarily focusing on the Twos and Threes because Ones don't typically require much coaxing, while the Fours and Fives are still probably beyond our reach.

From there, we can zoom in further to identify any connections we might already have with the Twos and Threes we've listed and discuss what partnership with them might actually look like. In this context, terms like "partnership" and "collaboration" actually aren't specific enough. The Collaboration Spectrum, developed by the Tamarack Institute,[10] offers us a more precise language for thinking and communicating about how we might choose to work with others.

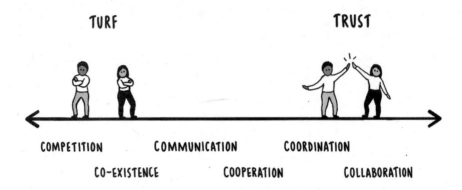

Figure 10.3: The Collaboration Spectrum.

Except for Competition, these six different ways of relating to other organizations are all arranged from the lowest level of involvement (on the left) to the highest (on the right). While we may understandably long for the intimacy of authentic Collaboration, Communication, Cooperation, and Coordination are often more practical.

Communication: One example of Communication is offering cross-promotional support. Your group might create a form on your website that related organizations can use to submit relevant news and events. In exchange for including them in your newsletter and social media posts, you might request that they periodically promote your activities to their members as well. Without much effort, both groups benefit from additional exposure to audiences they might not otherwise be able to reach.

Cooperation: Cooperation might look like partnering with another organization on a particular event. You might invite someone from another group to give a presentation or teach a workshop for your members. This enables the host to offer valuable content without having to produce it themselves, and provides the partnering organization with an opportunity to share their work with potential supporters. If the other organization also helps you promote your event, you might add their logo and website to the flier, and if you charge admission, you might split the revenue with them.

Coordination: Coordination refers to an ongoing partnership in which each group plays a particular role. In the case of Transition Sarasota's Suncoast Gleaning Project, we partner with farms that provide the produce and food banks that distribute it to those in need. Transition Sarasota simply supplies the missing link: the volunteers needed to harvest it. We don't tell the farms how to grow their vegetables or the food banks how to manage their distribution networks. Instead, we coordinate with each other, each organization contributing what it's best at.

Collaboration: In this context and elsewhere, Collaboration can be thought of as exploring the unknown together. If we're approaching a potential partner with a fixed idea about what we want them to do, that isn't really Collaboration and we should at least be honest about that. Serious problems can arise when partners are led to believe they will have a say over all aspects of a project when they actually won't.

After deciding what we want from a potential partner, we also need to think about what we can offer in return. This can be tangible (like money, volunteers, or expertise) or intangible (like visibility and recognition). However, it has to be something our partner will find to be of equal or greater value. This practice of defining mutual benefit is often referred to as creating a "value proposition." It's an exercise in putting yourself in the other organization's shoes.

If you haven't already, it's a good idea to do some research before meeting with potential partners, so you're aware of their current activities. You might even attend a few of their events to meet some of the people involved. Then, when you're in the same room together, err on the side of humility. Ask lots of questions and don't assume you have all the answers or that you're doing the other group a favor.

By engaging in mutually beneficial partnerships like this, we begin to shift culture away from the zero-sum mentality of competition that's so pervasive in our society. Instead of fighting over slices of a pie that's much too small for everyone to eat, we should work together to grow the size of the pie.

When I was living in Sarasota, a friend of mine tried to reserve a booth at her local farmers' market to sell veggies and fish from her backyard aquaponics farm. However, when she approached the market manager, she was told they already had too many farmers. We subsequently circulated a petition to try to convince the market manager otherwise, but to no avail. As a result, she was forced to shut down. Although the farmers' market where I live now has many times more farmers than the one my friend was trying to get into, it also has many times more customers, partly because it has more farmers and more options to choose from.

While Transition Sarasota never formally established a local foodshed coalition, as other communities have, our Eat Local Week Planning Committee functioned a lot like one. Every year, we'd invite all of the organizations and businesses that were listed in our Eat Local Guide, plus a handful of other allies, to cocreate it. Transition Sarasota convened the group, facilitated its monthly meetings, raised funds to support the overall effort, and handled the bulk of the promotion, but partners made all major decisions collectively, contributed their own events to the shared program, and kept whatever profits their events generated.

This kind of arrangement can benefit everyone involved. Other common examples are local independent business alliances and climate justice coalitions. Although these groups are often stewarded by one organization, any member can propose a new project and decisions are made democratically. Beyond simply partnering with other groups on an individual basis, we can gradually weave alliances, coalitions, and networks around whatever issues we're addressing.

Building Bridges Across Difference

While there are many painful divides in our society crying out to be bridged and healed, perhaps none is more important than the one between what we might call "people of privilege" (who tend to be wealthy and white) and "frontline communities" (which are disproportionately made up of People of Color). Centuries of genocide, slavery, colonization, oppression, and exploitation perpetrated by people of privilege against frontline communities has opened up a massive rift between these two groups, which is often filled with fear, anger, and distrust. Understandably, frontline communities tend to view people of privilege with skepticism, while I suspect many well-meaning people of privilege avoid interacting with frontline communities because they secretly fear being called out.

This is an especially important dynamic to consider in our current context because people of privilege, both here in the US and around the world, hold the vast majority of the wealth and power that could be used to bring about a just transition, while frontline communities continue to suffer the most from problems they did little or nothing to create. Given our history, I believe it's the responsibility of people of privilege to make the first move.

I know I haven't reached across this divide as much as I should have, not because I didn't want to but because I was afraid of perpetuating the harms that so many people like me have inflicted upon frontline communities in the past. Many have observed this same pattern unfold decade after decade: naive do-gooders parachuting in with big plans and promises, only to soak up much of the available funding and claim all of the credit without leaving anything of lasting value behind.

One thing I did right during my time with Transition Sarasota was to look for bridge builders. Even in Sarasota, which remains highly segregated, I would occasionally meet people with a rare talent for traversing these two worlds. Lou Murray, an elder Black man who had previously been a leader in the local food movement in Detroit, was one such person. As a result of Lou joining our Eat Local Week Planning Committee in 2015, Newtown Nation created their first annual Big Mama's Collard Green Festival, which continues to be one of their most popular events.

To prepare the ground for authentic partnership and collaboration, people of privilege need to first educate themselves about issues related to diversity and social justice, and commit to helping to bring about a more equitable future. This requires those of us who are accustomed to having our way to listen more than speak and voluntarily give up some of our own power. Even though we may not have directly created the inequalities that exist in our world today, this is what it takes to rebalance the scales of justice.

Conventional Diversity, Equity, and Inclusion efforts like affirmative hiring practices and mandatory educational programs are important, but they aren't sufficient to rebuild trust between frontline communities and people of privilege. To accomplish this, people of privilege need to actively demonstrate their solidarity with frontline communities by working together to serve their needs and showing up to support their leadership. This is how I believe we will build a more authentically diverse movement without colonizing or tokenizing.

The mainstream environmental movement here in the US has historically been made up almost entirely of people of privilege. As Van Jones observed in his 2008 book, *The Green Collar Economy*:

> [America's] environmental movement is almost explicitly segregated by race—the mainstream environmentalists are in one camp (mostly white) and the environmental justice activists are in another (made up almost entirely by people of color). Without assigning blame to anyone on either side, it is safe to say that the entire second wave of environmentalism has been less powerful, less perceptive, and less transformative than it might have been, if the leaders on both sides had been able to overcome the divisions.[11]

While significant progress has been made towards integrating movements for justice and sustainability here in the US over the past 15 years, there's obviously a lot more to do. To protect the most vulnerable, end systemic inequality, and bring people of privilege and frontline communities together in shared struggle, Jones recommends focusing on what he calls "the Fourth Quadrant": solutions that prioritize the needs of frontline communities while lowering greenhouse gas emissions and protecting nature for all. For Jones, this specifically means creating millions of good green jobs for low-income People of Color building out America's renewable energy infrastructure, but we can also think of the Fourth Quadrant more broadly as including all efforts that meaningfully advance both sustainability and justice.

Figure 10.4: Van Jones' Four Quadrants.[12]

There's really no reason why a lot more of this couldn't happen. Beyond merely protecting the planet for future generations, many regenerative solutions also have the effect of decentralizing wealth and power, which has the potential to lead to a much more equitable society. If we're able to communicate this effectively and back it up with action, we might finally bring people of privilege and frontline communities together to build a future that includes and celebrates everyone.

Integral Activism

While there's an obvious moral imperative to build bridges across race and class, they aren't the only divides preventing people from coming together. If we are to include everyone in our initiative and build an unstoppable movement, we must also learn how to connect across different cultures, religions, generations, and political ideologies.

Originally developed as "the emergent cyclical theory of adult human development" by psychology professor Clare Graves, Spiral Dynamics was introduced to the general public by Don Beck and Chris Cowan in their 1996 book of the same name,[13] and further popularized through the writings of Ken Wilber.[14] In its most basic form, Spiral Dynamics describes six "First-Tier" worldviews that have emerged in response to corresponding life conditions. It also identifies various levels of "Second-Tier" consciousness that transcend and include all the others.

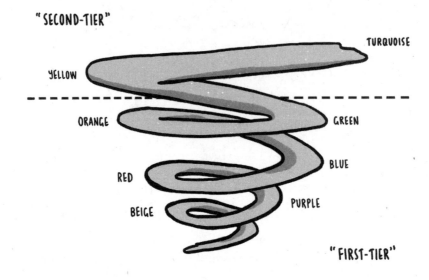

Figure 10.5: A conventional representation of Spiral Dynamics.

The reason why Beige, Purple, Red, Blue, Orange, and Green are referred to as First-Tier is simply because they all believe that they alone perceive reality accurately, while everyone else is basically deluded. In contrast, Second-Tier integral consciousness recognizes that each of these worldviews embodies a unique perspective and energy that's needed for the health of the whole. The integral activist seeks to weave all of these worldviews together in such a way that they are not only able to coexist, but actually complement and benefit each other.

There are good reasons why Spiral Dynamics is typically presented as a hierarchy of levels of consciousness, but this can be easily misconstrued as a way to pigeonhole others and look down on them from our imagined perch at the top. This is why I prefer to represent Spiral Dynamics as a round table around which representatives of each of the First-Tier worldviews are seated. This makes it clear that none is meant to be perceived as higher or lower, and it's only by placing the integral perspective at the center that we're able to come together as equals and allies.

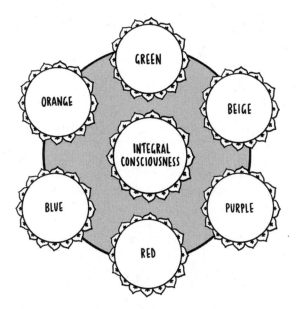

Figure 10.6: A non-hierarchical perspective on Spiral Dynamics.

Because all of the main proponents of Spiral Dynamics have given different descriptive names to each worldview, I've taken the liberty of doing the same here. In the following paragraphs, I'll attempt to characterize all six in greater detail and suggest how we might engage them in the work of Transition.

Survivalist (Beige): The Beige worldview is focused primarily on survival. We might see Beige reflected in those who are living on the streets, just struggling to get by, or caught up in the midst of a war or some other disaster. The strengths of Beige are that it's extremely pragmatic, resourceful, and determined. Like all worldviews, when Beige becomes too extreme or is applied in the wrong context, it becomes unhealthy and problematic. However, when it's properly balanced, it can make a valuable contribution to the entire spiral.

We might appeal to Beige by emphasizing Transition's ability to meet basic needs and strengthen local resilience. People who identify with Beige might be especially interested in the Great Reskilling. We might tell Beige that "because modern civilization is increasingly vulnerable to collapse and no one can survive alone, we need to prepare collectively now for the hard times that are coming."

Tribal (Purple): Purple can be seen in groups that are tightly bonded, like military units, sports teams, intentional communities, and religious cults. These groups all tend to have their own myths, rituals, and culture that set them apart from the rest of society. At its best, Purple greatly enriches our lives with meaning and satisfies our fundamental need for community.

Those with dominant Purple tendencies typically find themselves drawn to the Inner Transition. Transition Trainings can act as rites of passage, and visioning taps into Purple's rich imaginative capacities. We might entice Purple to join our movement by mentioning that "Transition is all about reconnecting with the Earth, each other, and ourselves. In this crazy world we've created, we've lost connection with what's truly important."

Heroic (Red): Red is the driving force behind warriors and empire builders. While it may only surge to the forefront when we're faced with an acute threat, it can also become an entire way of life when we're forced to endure too much harm and unsafety for too long. Red can be aggressive and cruel, but also has the potential to inspire others with its toughness and courage.

Describing Transition as an epic adventure and a historic challenge of global proportions deeply appeals to Red. Although Red may not have the patience to sit through long process-heavy meetings, it's likely to be among the first to step into action. We might rally Red by proclaiming "Transition is the Great Work of our time! By rising to meet these monumental challenges, we will unlock our greatest potential and shape the future for generations to come."

Traditional (Blue): Blue is most often found in rural communities and mainstream religions. It generally values law and order, hard work and frugality, and respect for established authorities. Although Blue's conservatism can cause it to stubbornly cling to the past and try to impose its ideas of right and wrong on others, its commitment to being a good neighbor and living in a righteous way can be positively channeled towards regeneration.

While Blue is more likely to support incremental changes than try to overthrow the system, it's a hard worker and a powerful ally. We might explain Transition to Blue by observing that "it's basically about local food, local energy, local economy, and local community. We're becoming producers again instead of just consumers, and creating a better world for our children and grandkids."

Modern (Orange): Orange is the unofficial worldview of the Industrial Growth Society. As such, it's mainly concerned with rationality, achievement, and progress. While it's most obvious in the realms of business, politics, science, and technology, Orange pervades all of modern civilization and remains its dominant paradigm. With its unprecedented power to reshape the world, Orange has the potential to create massive harm or good, depending on how its prodigious energies are directed.

For Transition to be successful in an Orange world, it needs more Orange people who know how to run organizations, think strategically, and scale up. Orange might be intrigued by Transition's sophisticated understanding of our global context, complex strategy, and impressive metrics. It might also respond enthusiastically to the many opportunities for innovation and entrepreneurship inherent in Transition. We might suggest to Orange that "life with less oil could be preferable to the present, if we plan ahead with imagination and creativity."[15]

Post-Modern (Green): Green is passionately devoted to personal development, social justice, and sustainability. It earnestly believes in peace and love and actively seeks to remedy environmental imbalances, exploitation, and inequality. Green is wonderful, but it goes too far when it rejects all of the other worldviews in favor of its own strict ideological purity. In fact, Green is only possible because Beige, Purple, Red, Blue, and Orange also exist.

Most progressive activists tend to be rooted in Green. Green is naturally attracted to Transition's vision of a just and regenerative future as well as its collaborative, creative, and decentralized approach. We might simply share with Green that "Transition is a global movement of communities coming together to reimagine and rebuild our world."

Whether it was intentionally designed this way or not, Transition is an integral movement. There are many different doorways through which many different kinds of people can enter and get involved. Transition also acknowledges that we don't have to agree with others on everything to work together on the issues we do agree on. This echoes the perspective of Clare Graves himself, who said: "Damn it all, a person has a right to be. A person has a right to be what he is. He shouldn't have to change to get your work done."[16]

Nevertheless, in practice, Transition has too closely associated itself with Green, with its impossible idealism, reactionary aversion to money and power, and tendency to get bogged down in endless processing. Only by incorporating more Beige, Purple, Red, Blue, and Orange into our movement will we be able to bring about the unprecedented coming together of society that our current crisis demands.

We can do this because we carry the entire spiral within us. Regardless of which colors are currently most prominent in our lives, if we look carefully enough, we'll see that there are always circumstances that call for the practicality of Beige, the mysticism of Purple, the heroism of Red, the traditionalism of Blue, the industriousness of Orange, and the egalitarianism of Green. If we can embrace all of these colors within ourselves, we will be able to recognize how they manifest in the world and intuitively know the right mix to apply in any given situation.

During my time with Transition Colorado, I organized a workshop on Spiral Dynamics with local Permaculture teacher, farmer, and healer Marco Lam. Towards the end of the afternoon, he facilitated a brilliant exercise for practicing integral activism. It begins with one participant proposing an idea for an event or project to a council of six others, representing each of the First-Tier worldviews. They listen and offer feedback. Then, after the first round, the proposer is invited to adjust their proposal as many times as necessary until they finally win support from everyone. I suspect this same activity could also be done individually by playing all seven roles yourself.

Practical Projects

To be truly radical is to make hope possible
rather than despair convincing.

— Raymond Williams[1]

If we want a just and regenerative future, we're going to have to build it ourselves. Governments and businesses can and should support these efforts, but they can't and won't bring about all of the changes that are needed by themselves. Throughout history, whenever radical transformation has occurred, grassroots movements have led the way. Our business and political leaders may lag behind for a while, but they eventually have to learn to follow or end up losing our support.

When I attended the Global Climate Action Summit in San Francisco in 2018, the big news was that Jerry Brown had recently announced California would become carbon neutral by 2045. While I was encouraged by the Governor of the fifth largest economy in the world making such an ambitious commitment, I had to wonder: how is that actually going to happen? There are 39.5 million people in the Golden State, and short of unprecedented government intervention (which I think we should all be wary of), how will every individual and household, block and neighborhood, city and town, and business and industry become carbon neutral?

To do this, we need to bring our lofty ideas down to Earth, put them into practice, and help them to scale. By setting up and running practical projects, we can create "microcosms of hope" that inspire others to action.

While the main purpose of practical projects is to solve pressing problems and make our world a better place to live, the value of their many indirect benefits shouldn't be underestimated. Practical projects also offer opportunities for people to build confidence in taking action, learn how to work with others, and acquire valuable skills.

Although practical projects are clearly the most exciting and visible aspect of the Transition process, their success is dependent on all of the other ingredients we have explored so far. Before launching practical projects, we need to understand the issues we're trying to address, have a vision of the change we want to create, prepare ourselves to step into leadership, call together a group of committed allies, and engage our wider community. We could call this "the iceberg theory of evolutionary change."

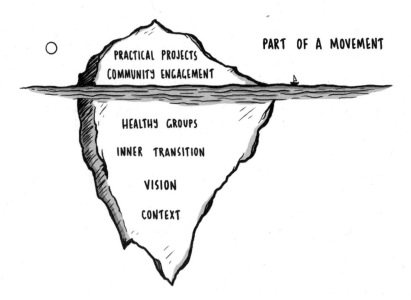

Figure 11.1: The iceberg theory of evolutionary change.

Practical projects also offer opportunities to learn more about the change-making process itself. If we've never really tried to change anything, we might assume it's a lot simpler and easier than it is. For this reason, it's wise to experiment with making changes in our own personal lives before involving others. By doing so, we'll quickly realize that living up to our ideals is impossible to do perfectly in a society that's deeply imperfect. Most of us live in places where the best option is usually the lesser of two evils. In all of the choices we make, we're forced to straddle two worlds: our present reality and our future vision. As challenging as this is, it's still possible to take meaningful steps forward into the better world we imagine.

Food: One of the most impactful actions we can take as individuals and households is simply to grow a garden. Producing our own food is an accessible and empowering first step towards freeing ourselves from dependence on the Industrial Growth Society. Through the humble act of gardening, we reconnect with nature, improve health, save money, reduce consumption of natural resources, sequester carbon, build soil, increase biodiversity, and strengthen local food security, all at the same time.

If you're a renter, you could grow in containers, and if you don't have space where you live, you could join a community garden. Costs for starting a garden are typically minimal and decrease over time, while the size of your harvests will increase along with your knowledge. If you've never grown your own food before, there are countless books, YouTube tutorials, and gardening groups that would be happy to teach you how.

Because few gardeners grow everything they eat, we should also think about how we source the rest of our food. Simply by shopping at a nearby farmers' market once a week or purchasing a Community Supported Agriculture share,[2] we can support local farmers and promote the growth of local food systems. While local organic produce is typically more expensive, an increasing number of programs are popping up all over the US and around the world to subsidize the purchasing power of low-income individuals and families.[3]

We might also consider eating a plant-based diet, composting at home, harvesting rainwater, recycling greywater, and using drip irrigation in our gardens. Once we've mastered the basics, we can extend ourselves further by saving seeds, keeping bees and chickens, preserving produce, and sharing our surplus with friends and neighbors. Developing these skills might even lead you to start your own local food enterprise, such as an edible landscaping service or a communal kitchen.

Economy: For those of us who already have way too much stuff, reducing our consumption requires little sacrifice and can have significant benefits. Simply by not buying items we don't really need, investing in products that last, learning to repair what's damaged or broken, and shopping second-hand, we can save money while shrinking our ecological footprint and decluttering our minds. We can also find ways to share more, informally through gift and barter economies as well as formally through programs like time banks, coworking spaces, and libraries of things.

On the rare occasion we need to buy something new, we should prioritize locally owned, independent businesses over corporations and chain stores, which tend to siphon wealth out of communities. In contrast, when you spend money at a local business, a much higher percentage of each dollar continues to circulate locally, creating more jobs, raising wages, improving working conditions, and providing additional revenue for public services.[4] Where they can be found, credit unions and worker-owned cooperatives in particular deserve our support.

When we patronize these businesses, we're essentially voting for more vibrant, sustainable, and equitable local economies. Likewise, when we purchase products that are made from simple natural ingredients and sold without excessive packaging, we're voting for fewer toxic chemicals and less waste. As more people buy sustainable products, they generally become cheaper and more widely available. At this point, I hope it goes without saying that single-use plastic bags and water bottles should be avoided completely.

Possibly our most difficult task in this area is take a hard look at what we're doing for a living and ask ourselves if it's contributing to the world we want. Of course, most people don't have the ability to change jobs or shift careers instantly, but if we're working for a company that's actively harming people or nature, we should at least begin considering our options.

Energy: Although solar panels and electric cars are the most well-known strategies for reducing dependence on fossil fuels, they aren't necessarily the most important or impactful. Even if you can afford the upfront cost of a photovoltaic system, it's recommended that you maximize energy conservation and efficiency first. Here in the US, most power companies offer free home energy audits, providing professional advice for lowering your energy bills. While sealing cracks in windows and doors, fine-tuning your thermostat settings, adding insulation, and switching to LED lights may not be as exciting as installing a brand-new solar array, these actions don't cost much (if anything) and can provide substantial savings over time.

Similarly, even if we can afford an electric car, we should consider first whether we could move closer to the places we frequently go, and walk, bike, or take public transit instead. An increasing number of communities have car-sharing services that can be used to travel to out-of-the-way locations and transport heavy loads, making it a lot easier to get rid of your car altogether. It's an inconvenient truth, but electric cars take a lot of energy and materials to build, create traffic and waste, and still typically run on electricity produced by coal or fracked gas.

Because long-distance travel is one of our most carbon-intensive activities, it merits special attention. One cross-country or international trip can undo a year's worth of diligent efforts to reduce our environmental footprint. Although flying is sometimes the only practical way to visit distant family and friends, jetting off to a tropical island for a short vacation is no longer morally defensible. Whether we're looking for culture, relaxation, or beauty, we should be able to meet those needs much closer to home. As my friend Richard Dart said: "Once you've had a taste of real community, a trip to Milan pales in comparison!"

Community: As human beings, we're wired for community. We all need it and suffer greatly in its absence. The fragmentation of traditional communities that has taken place over the past few centuries has offered us greater freedom, but has also left many of us feeling increasingly isolated and unwell. While single-family houses, gated communities, and automatic garage-door openers provide a modicum of security, comfort, and convenience for the individual, the separation they create has negative consequences for society: psychologically, economically, and ecologically.

Although we shouldn't underestimate the power of far-flung allies, online community is no substitute for in-person connections. We can begin cultivating place-based community simply by reaching out to our neighbors and inviting them to a potluck or block party, then setting up a mailing list or social media group to communicate, organize future events, and exchange needs and offers on an ongoing basis.

The most powerful step we can take in this area is to join an intentional community. Most aren't at all like the chaotic and insular hippy communes of the past. Rather, they are rooted in broadly held values like cooperation, mutual aid, and sustainability, and welcome people of all backgrounds and beliefs. They are also usually more affordable and use much less energy and resources than conventional housing arrangements. Intentional communities are like microcosms of the larger society we're trying to create, with their own systems of food, economy, energy, and governance that we can participate in, learn from, and help shape. By living in community, we prepare ourselves practically, socially, and psychologically for a relocalized and interdependent future.

Anatomy of a Great First Project

When selecting which practical projects to launch into our wider community, we should always be guided by our community's needs and interests; our group's vision, mission, and goals; and the opportunities that are currently available to us. To choose wisely among the options that remain, we have to think strategically.

To help activists evaluate the merits and improve the design of their practical projects, I've developed a framework I call "Anatomy of a Great First Project." As you'll see, the following eight principles are based on why I believe Transition Sarasota's Suncoast Gleaning Project has been so successful.

1. It addresses a real need: The first reason I believe our gleaning project has been so successful is because it addresses a real need. Even in a relatively wealthy county like Sarasota, around 10 percent of all residents are considered "food insecure."[5] While local food banks have long existed to serve this demographic, when we launched the Suncoast Gleaning Project in 2010, the vast majority of what they distributed wasn't very healthy. For example, if you were dependent on emergency food assistance and wanted fruits and vegetables to feed your family, the best you could probably hope for was some sugary fruit juice and soggy canned vegetables. By donating tens of thousands of pounds of local organic produce every year to local food banks, Transition Sarasota was able to significantly improve quality of life for those struggling the most economically in our area.

2. It harnesses existing energy: As I've alluded to before, the founding of Transition Sarasota happened to coincide with a major surge of interest, both locally and worldwide, in regenerative agriculture and local food systems. As a result, more and more farms, farmers' markets, and community gardens were popping up every year in Sarasota around that time. Rather than swimming against the current by trying to address an issue people didn't already care about, we decided to harness this existing momentum. As a result, it was relatively easy for us to find volunteers, partners, and funders to support the Suncoast Gleaning Project.

3. It fits your group's capacity: Many groups make the mistake of taking on projects that are so big and demanding they're unable to do anything else. Because everything tends to take much longer and require a lot more work than initially expected, we should be careful to avoid overwhelming our capacity. In the beginning, it makes sense to start small, focus on harvesting low-hanging fruit, and play to our strengths as organizers. If our Suncoast Gleaning Project had to grow and distribute all of the produce we donated, it wouldn't have been a great first project. However, because we were already connected with farms that had surplus produce and food banks with extensive distribution systems, all we needed to do was provide the missing link. This meant that, during the project's first few years, I was able to coordinate it in only 5 to 10 hours a week, which left plenty of time for other pursuits.

4. It gets as many people as possible involved: The more people your practical projects involve, the better. While gleanings typically require dozens of volunteers to harvest everything that's available, this is actually more of a strength than a burden. By working together in the fields, gleaners form friendships and build community, develop skills and knowledge, and often discover a newfound sense of empowerment. As multiple pallets stack up with crates full of produce that would have otherwise been wasted, many are shocked and inspired to see how much a small group of volunteers can accomplish in just a few short hours.

5. It's a win for everyone: Sometimes somebody has to lose for someone else to win, but practical projects that offer a win for everyone demonstrate change isn't always a zero-sum game. The Suncoast Gleaning Project provides small farmers with a tax deduction equal to the value of the produce they donate, offers those who depend on emergency food assistance an option for healthier eating, and invites volunteers to take home a bag full of produce for themselves. All of this is achieved simply by rescuing crops that would have otherwise been tilled into the soil. Particularly in wealthy countries and communities, there are many opportunities to transform waste into a valuable resource.

6. It makes for a great story: The Suncoast Gleaning Project makes for a great story because it's somewhat unusual, unequivocally positive, photogenic, and easy to understand. In addition to images, videos, and testimonials, it can be helpful to collect hard metrics from your practical projects. It's hugely powerful to be able to say that we've now donated over half a million pounds of produce. As a result, the Suncoast Gleaning Project has been the subject of dozens of local TV and radio segments, newspaper and magazine articles. This has served to educate the general public about issues related to food insecurity, local food systems, and regenerative agriculture, while raising awareness about Transition Sarasota as an organization.

7. It can be scaled up and replicated: Although the Suncoast Gleaning Project began with just one farm that I was personally connected to, it gradually expanded over the years to include ongoing relationships with several other local farms, the gleaning of residential fruit trees, and rescuing surplus produce from local farmers' markets. It has also inspired and informed similar efforts by other organizations. At least partly due to our influence, our community food bank invested in two large trucks specifically for distributing fresh produce a few years after we started working together, and in 2016, the Florida Department of Agriculture used Transition Sarasota as a model for piloting new gleaning projects statewide. In this way, the ripples of our practical projects can extend far beyond their origins, acting as catalysts for even more widespread change.

8. It stacks many functions: I've borrowed this final principle from Permaculture. "Stacking functions" refers to the ability of one highly strategic action to bring about multiple benefits at the same time. It's like the work of a skilled acupuncturist, who sticks a sharp needle in one spot to positively influence the health of an entire body. Because Transition Sarasota's Suncoast Gleaning Project has embodied all of the other principles described above, it has been a hugely successful first project.

Other Great First Projects

First projects can make or break an initiative. If they don't catch on and establish a sense of momentum fairly quickly, that can be the end of everything. However, if they succeed, they can act as a foundation upon which bigger and more impactful projects can be built in the future.

All great first projects incorporate many (if not all) of the principles outlined above. In this section, we'll focus on five that are commonly undertaken early on in the Transition process. If we had more space, I might also discuss community asset mapping, retrofitting low-income homes for maximum energy efficiency, and setting up community food forests, plant nurseries, tool libraries, and bike shops.

Permablitzes: Originally developed by the Permaculture Movement, permablitzes bring together groups of volunteers to establish new gardens, often ripping out lawns and transforming them into edible landscapes in a single day. Homeowners typically pay for any supplies that are needed and prepare a meal to share. Volunteers frequently earn credits that make them eligible to host a permablitz at their home in the future. While everyone always learns by doing, permablitzes sometimes double as reskilling workshops on topics like installing rainwater collection systems or building a chicken coop.

In 2008, just as Transition Milwaukee was getting started, one of its members, Gretchen Mead, proposed a project that would draw on the proud legacy of the victory garden movement here in the US, which inspired 20 million families to grow at least some of their own food during World War II.[6] With Transition Milwaukee's support, Mead launched her Victory Garden Initiative (VGI) the following year. Nearly 100 volunteers turned out for their first annual Memorial Day Blitz to install 40 edible gardens in front yards and backyards, at schools and churches, and on rooftops throughout the city.

VGI has now installed more than 5,000 gardens all over Milwaukee, with a focus on serving low-income residents and neighborhoods. It also currently manages the Victory Garden Urban Farm, which gives away all of its produce, and offers educational tours and workshops for hundreds of kids and adults each year. Inspired by VGI, Milwaukee's Environmental Collaboration Office established its own HOME GR/OWN initiative to transform vacant lots into gardens, and two other nonprofits have since formed in the Greater Milwaukee area to meet the unprecedented demand for edible garden installations that VGI created.[7]

Repair cafes: The repair cafe movement started in the Netherlands in 2009 and has since spread to more than 2,600 communities in dozens of countries worldwide.[8] The basic idea is to connect people who need things fixed with those who have the tools, knowledge, and skills to fix them. Repair cafes not only save people money and keep trash out of landfills. By requiring participants to sit with the person fixing their item, they also facilitate community building and reskilling.

Common items mended include clothes, furniture, electronic appliances, bicycles, pots and pans, toys, and jewelry. In its most basic form, cafe organizers simply procure a suitable venue, pick a date and time, and send out an invitation. However, many repair cafes have evolved to provide additional perks for participants, such as live music, educational classes, seed swaps, haircuts, and massages.

Transition Pasadena created one of the first repair cafes in the US, and many other Transition Initiatives have followed their example, including Transition Berkeley, Transition Houston, Transition Howard County, Sustainable Charlotte Vermont, and Woodstock NY Transition.[9] In a time when so much is designed to be used up, thrown out, and bought again, repair cafes remind us this isn't the only way. By relying more on community and less on corporations, we can start to fix our own problems, become more skilled and connected, and serve as better stewards of nature.

Time banks: Although time banks are often classified as a form of local currency, they are better thought of as a type of mutual aid network or as an operating system for what Edgar Cahn calls "the core economy."[10] The core economy includes many services that people usually aren't paid for and don't count towards a country's Gross Domestic Product, but are essential for the healthy functioning of any society. Examples include caring for the young and elderly, helping neighbors in need, volunteering for charitable organizations, and sharing our passions and talents with others. Time banks help draw out these hidden resources, give them value, and facilitate their exchange.

Most time banks utilize an online platform that looks similar to Craigslist, with its directory of offers and requests, but operates according to a very different set of values. The most well-known (and controversial) aspect of time banking is that everyone's time is worth one hour, whether it's spent walking someone's dog or offering professional medical advice. Once the person receiving a service credits the account of the person providing it, that person can then spend their "time dollars" on anything that's available on the platform.

It's fairly easy to set up a time bank and get started using one of several platforms that have been designed for this purpose. The biggest challenge is maintaining its use over time. The most successful time banks organize events to bring in new people, foster a sense of community, train them how to use the system, and actively encourage them to post offers and requests. Some even sponsor their own projects, like the Dane County Time Bank in Wisconsin, which has over 6,000 members and pays teens in time dollars to serve on their local youth court.

Solarize initiatives: Most projects aimed at increasing local renewable energy production are costly and technically complex, requiring major changes in government or utility company policies. Solarize initiatives are a notable exception. They typically start with a local government, nonprofit organization, or community group partnering with a solar energy installer and negotiating a bulk discount on photovoltaic systems. Then, if a certain number of people sign up for the program by a deadline, everybody receives the bulk discount on top of other incentives and rebates.

While it's true that many people can't afford a solar array even with this kind of assistance, solarize initiatives encourage those households who can to stop sitting on the fence. By rallying these Early Adopters to invest in solar, they have the potential to bring down the price for everyone and send a powerful message that the energy transition is finally happening. Ultimately, we need every tool in our tool box to end our dangerous dependence on fossil fuels.

The Energy Group of Transition Town Media (Pennsylvania) started their Solarize Greater Media campaign in 2015, and over the next two years, recruited hundreds of people to join. In partnership with the Delaware Valley Regional Planning Commission and the Delaware County Planning Department, solar systems were installed on 43 homes, generating a combined 300kW and saving participating households up to 20 percent of the cost. Transition Town Media's efforts helped their community earn recognition from the US Department of Energy as a solar-friendly town and led them to consult with other nearby communities, including Philadelphia's Energy Authority, which started Solarize Philly.[11]

Transition Streets: Transition Streets was initially developed by Transition Town Totnes, where it saved 550 participating households an average of $900 a year and reduced their carbon footprints by 1.3 tons annually. Transition US adapted this program in 2015 and recruited a dozen initiatives across eight states to pilot it. Since then, many others, both affiliated and unaffiliated with the Transition Movement, have facilitated Transition Streets in their local communities.[12]

Over the course of seven sessions, the Transition Streets Handbook[13] guides small groups of neighbors and community members in taking action to produce less waste, reduce energy and water consumption, and adopt a more sustainable diet. It also offers participants a valuable opportunity to get to know each other better and bond over their shared interest in Transition, which frequently leads to ongoing relationships and additional collaborations.

Some initiatives have developed creative ways to use Transition Streets, such as Transition Fort Collins, which used it as the basis for a Green Renters program they taught through Colorado State University, and Transition Albany (California), which employed it as a strategy to encourage residents to help implement their city's climate action plan. For its part, Transition US has subsequently created Transition Streets on a Budget and Transition Streets: Water-Saving Edition for drought-prone areas, as well as a similar program focused on neighborhood emergency preparedness called Ready Together.[14]

System-Changing Strategies

If our first projects prove successful, we can harness the momentum they've generated to scale up, which at this point is simply taking the next natural step. We're not talking about franchising a Starbucks or creating an everything app. Our initiatives are also not in danger of growing too large anytime soon. Although we may not feel ready to scale up yet, we should try to lean into this challenge when it comes.

There are several different ways we can scale up. We can teach others how to replicate our successes, expand existing projects, or attempt to implement more ambitious system-changing strategies as our capacity and confidence increases. We can also scale up by catalyzing working groups, forming coalitions, and merging multiple projects into thematic campaigns with a central unifying goal.

When Transition Sarasota simultaneously launched its Eat Local Guide and first annual Eat Local Week around Earth Day 2011, we began to bundle all of our local food-related activities (including our Suncoast Gleaning Project, reskilling workshops, and educational events) into an overarching Local Food Shift Campaign. What tied all of this together was a goal of shifting Sarasota County's food purchases at least 10 percent towards local sources within 10 years. While 10 percent might not sound like much, the same 2006 study I cited in chapter 5 found that only 0.7 percent of the food consumed in Sarasota County at that time was being sourced locally, so 10 percent represented a more than tenfold increase. We were also betting that by the time people got to 10 percent, many would be enjoying it so much that they would be inspired to do a lot more.

This same progression from smaller projects to bigger projects to multi-faceted campaigns can happen around other topics as well. For example, if your group is focused on energy, you might start by training volunteers to weatherize local homes and businesses, then establish a community-owned renewable energy company, and later get involved in updating your community's climate action plan. All of this (and more) could be organized around a goal of reducing greenhouse gas emissions by a certain percentage by a certain year. Similarly, if your group is focused on economy, you might start with a buy local campaign, then launch a local complementary currency and a local investment network in an effort to move a specific amount of money into your local economy over a specific period of time.

Strategy is always important to make the best possible use of limited resources. In the beginning, we have to be somewhat opportunistic, but even later on, once we've developed the funding, capacity, connections, and expertise to undertake whatever projects we want, we should still be selective. We should try to think like enlightened community planners, asking ourselves and others what infrastructure is needed most to transform entire systems as well as what needs to be done now to create the conditions for subsequent changes to occur.

To inspire hope that ordinary people such as ourselves can bring about meaningful change, I've included brief snapshots below of some of the largest and most successful systems-changing strategies I know. Because these kinds of stories are not often reported on in the mainstream media, we need to do everything in our power to get them out as far and wide as possible.

Regional food hubs: Networks for the aggregation and distribution of local and regional produce were commonplace only a century ago, but many were dismantled during the process of economic globalization. One group that's been trying to bring theirs back is the Belgian Transition Initiative, Liége en Transition. In 2013, they helped establish Ceinture Aliment-Terre Liégeoise (CATL), "The Liége Food Belt." Since then, CATL has woven together a powerful network of 15 local food cooperatives, including several farms and grocery stores, organizations dedicated to preserving agricultural lands and sharing farm machinery, a bicycle delivery service, two bakeries, two wineries, and a brewery.

CATL supports them all by organizing events, creating educational resources, facilitating collaboration and resource sharing, and helping to raise millions of Euros for startups and expansions. It has also established a partnership with the City of Liège to lease public lands to local growers, helped form a district-wide food policy council, and regularly consults with schools about sourcing locally. According to CATL, which maps local producers on their website, all of this has led to a doubling of market gardeners in their area over the past decade, with much more still to come.[15]

Community-owned renewable energy companies: Many Transition Initiatives, from Fujino, Japan, to London, England, have started their own community-owned renewable energy companies.[16] These entities typically raise funds by offering shares to local investors, some of whom pitch in as little as a few hundred dollars, then use those funds to purchase, install, and maintain solar photovoltaic arrays and wind turbines. The community as a whole benefits from increased renewable energy production, and small local investors, instead of utility company executives and shareholders, reap the financial benefits.

Although it's not the largest community-owned renewable energy company a Transition Initiative has established, Brixton Energy might be my favorite. In partnership with Repowering London, they have so far installed three large solar arrays on public housing, specifically to lower the energy bills of their community's most economically challenged residents. The biggest might be Bath & West Community Energy, which has raised £22.5 million to date and implemented 34 community energy projects totaling 13.35 MW, enough to power 4,500 homes.

Local currencies: Many Transition Initiatives have also started local complementary currencies.[17] Because they can only be spent at local businesses, they keep wealth circulating locally instead of being sent back to corporate headquarters. Local currencies remind those who use them of the benefits of shopping locally and serve as powerful symbols of community pride. The Brixton Pound's colorful £10 note, which features hometown hero David Bowie as Aladdin Sane, has been celebrated around the world.

At its peak in 2015, the Bristol Pound was the UK's largest local currency, with £800,000 in circulation and 280 local businesses accepting it. That year, Rob Hopkins wrote that it "combines printed notes, an Open Source Pay-by-Text system, and integration with the local credit union. It's accepted as payment on city buses, and the City Council pays part of its staff's salary in the currency. The mayor also takes his full salary in Bristol Pounds."[18] Residents could withdraw Bristol Pounds from ATMs throughout the city and use them to pay their local taxes and energy bills. While the Bristol Pound was officially retired in 2021, the team behind it is already working on their next iteration: Bristol Pay.

Local investment networks: Of the tens of trillions of dollars invested in stock markets worldwide, not a single dollar currently flows to local businesses. Local investment networks seek to convince investors to take at least some of their money out of speculative markets (where it may be helping to fund fossil fuel companies and weapons manufacturers) and put it to work supporting local businesses they know and believe in. Loans facilitated through these networks are typically low-interest, and because there is a direct relationship between the lender and borrower, agreements can be revised as needed.

Local 20/20, a Transition Initiative in Port Townsend, Washington, co-ordinates a Local Investing Opportunities Network (LION) that has served as a model for many similar efforts around the world.[19] Since 2012, it has catalyzed over $10.5 million of investment into 96 local businesses. Recipients have included a farm and cidery, a bicycle repair shop, an independent movie theater, and Washington's oldest grocery store. During the height of the pandemic, LION investors generously provided 47 borrowers with $1.8 million of debt relief. LION's latest project is a partnership with the Housing Solutions Network to fund affordable workforce housing in Jefferson County.

Community land trusts: The first community land trust in the US, New Communities Inc., was founded in 1969 by Black farmers and civil rights activists in Southwest Georgia as a way to acquire land and hold it in common in perpetuity. Although community land trusts remain a little-known strategy for ensuring permanently affordable housing, they are basically just a specific type of 501(c)(3) nonprofit. The organization raises the funds and owns the land, ensures each project stays true to its stated mission, and typically offers 99-year "ground leases" to residents. Residents own the homes they build and have representation on the nonprofit's board of directors, along with volunteer community members and subject area experts.

Dishmagu Humboldt is a community land trust founded in 2020 by the Wiyot Tribe of Northern California in partnership with local Transition Initiative Cooperation Humboldt. Organized around four main areas of focus (Land Back, Affordable Housing Creation, Workforce Development, and Environmental and Cultural Restoration), it aims to establish eco-villages that provide low-income housing, offer apprenticeship programs, and incubate worker-owned cooperatives. Its first major project, Jaroujiji Youth Housing, which will convert an office building and two single-family homes into 39 housing units for homeless youth, has already been supported by a $14 million grant from the State of California.[20]

Community-based redevelopment: In Totnes, England, where the Transition Movement started, they've taken on bigger and bigger projects over the past 18 years. The biggest of all is probably Atmos Totnes. In 2012, Transition Town Totnes helped found the Totnes Community Development Society (TCDS), which signed an agreement in 2014 to redevelop a derelict 8.6-acre industrial site in the center of town. The following year, TCDS held 20 public consultation sessions to solicit community input, receiving more than 4,000 individual contributions. The resulting design included 62 affordable housing units, 37 retirement homes, a 58-bed "eco-hotel," an arts and music venue, a health and wellness center, 76,000 square feet of workspace, and a local foods cafe, all owned by the community and powered by 100 percent renewable energy.[21]

Although this plan was approved by 86 percent of local voters in 2019 and TCDS secured enough funding to purchase the property, just as the deal was about to close, the owner sold the site behind their back to another buyer. Heartbroken but unwilling to surrender, those who had worked on this project for many years formed the Atmos for Totnes campaign in 2021. They collected 750 objections to the new owner's development plan, leading to its rejection in 2023. While the outcome still remains uncertain, I'm betting on Atmos Totnes to win. When a community claims its power to dream and design its own future like this, it becomes a force of nature that's nearly impossible to stop.

Municipalities in Transition: Transition Initiatives also frequently partner with their local governments to great effect. In just a few years, the Municipalities in Transition project collected 72 case studies of these kinds of impactful collaborations from all over the world. While gaining political influence at state, national, and international levels tends to be much more difficult, it's not beyond the realm of possibility, especially if we work together as a movement.

Ungersheim, France, which calls itself the world's first Transition Village, is an example of what can happen when a local government puts its full support behind this kind of effort. Inspired by watching the documentary film *In Transition 1.0*,[22] Ungersheim's Mayor, Jean-Claude Mench, subsequently rallied his entire government around the idea of Transition. In 2012, they published a 21-point plan [23] and immediately started putting it into action. Since then, Ungersheim has become a Fair Trade Town, banned pesticides and herbicides, campaigned to shut down a nearby nuclear power plant, launched a local currency called The Radish, created an Atlas of Biodiversity, converted a former mining site into a nature preserve and park, and switched to 100 percent organic school meals. They have also built the largest solar farm in their region, which provides electricity for 10,000 residents (five times the village's entire population), and have made public lands and facilities available for an ecovillage, a 20-acre organic farm, and two communal kitchens.

Part of a Movement

*Guided by simple rules, starling murmurations can react to their
environment as a group without a central leader orchestrating
their choices; in any instant, any part of the flock can transform
the movement of the whole flock.*

— adrienne maree brown, *Emergent Strategy* [1]

Without practical projects on the ground in local communities, we have
nothing. However, the work of one local initiative, no matter how impressive, is still just a drop in the proverbial bucket. To tip the balance of the
future decisively towards regeneration, we need to weave thousands of
impactful initiatives together into an unstoppable movement.

While there are many organizations that coordinate chapters of a wider
movement, the approach taken by the international Transition Network is
fairly unusual. Instead of pushing directives from the top down, it seeks to
listen to and serve the needs of the grassroots. Instead of requiring conformity, it encourages innovation. Instead of acting alone, it sees itself as part
of a much larger movement of movements.

The structure of the Transition Movement is best understood as a fractal
"holarchy," a series of nested circles in which each circle is autonomous
and self-organizing within its stated scope and domain, while also being
accountable in two directions: both towards the larger circles it's a part of as
well as the smaller circles it supports. Transition Initiatives are supported
in many areas of the world by regional and national Transition Hubs, some
of which have merged into more expansive Territories by geography or

language. Hubs and Territories are supported at the international level by Transition Network, the UK-based nonprofit, and the Hubs Group, which was established in 2017 to act as a more representative body for the global movement.

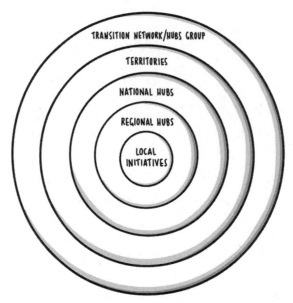

Figure 12.1: Transition Movement structure.

There are currently 26 regional and national hubs listed on Transition Network's global map: 19 in Europe, 2 in North America (the US and Mexico), 2 in South America (Colombia and Brazil), 1 in Asia (Japan), 1 in the Middle East (Israel), and 1 in Australia. The five main functions of Transition Hubs are to inspire, encourage, connect, train, and support.

Inspire: Hubs seek to inspire individuals and organizations throughout their geographical area by promoting the Transition vision and sharing stories of positive change. By promoting the Transition vision, hubs help people imagine a better future, and by sharing stories, they offer examples of what can be done. In a 2019 review of studies on climate change communications, Benjamin Ryan of the *New York Times*[2] concluded that stories like the ones I shared in the previous chapter tend to be much more effective in catalyzing change than fear-based, moralistic appeals.

Encourage: Hubs encourage action by developing programs local initiatives can use and participate in. Examples of programs initiatives can use include Transition Streets and Ready Together. Examples of programs initiatives can participate in include the annual Community Resilience Challenge Transition US previously promoted in partnership with Daily Acts, and a Pop Up Tomorrow international week of action organized by Transition Network in 2019.

Connect: Hubs connect Transitioners with each other, both online and in person, to facilitate peer-to-peer learning, mentoring, and support. This is commonly done by creating maps of Transition Initiatives, organizing meetings and conferences, and hosting communities of practice around shared interests. Because every group that's part of the Transition Movement shares the same basic understanding and approach, it's easier for Transition leaders to learn from each other. Connecting Transition Initiatives in this way also helps us feel less alone in our local work.

Train: Hubs train community leaders by offering courses and workshops designed to share best practices and replicable models. To lead a local Transition Initiative, groups must be able to communicate about Transition in a way that engages and inspires, work well with a wide variety of people, think strategically, organize impactful events and practical projects, and build momentum and capacity over time. However, most who step into leadership roles in the Transition Movement have never done anything like this before and don't automatically come equipped with all of these skills.

Support: Hubs also support Transition Initiatives by providing practical and technical assistance. They offer fiscal sponsorship for unincorporated groups, share technology platforms and professional services, engage in collaborative fundraising efforts, help to mediate conflicts, and promote the activities of local initiatives. Here as elsewhere, the prime directive of Transition Hubs is not to control local initiatives but to do whatever is needed to help them to thrive.

The State of the Movement

After nearly two decades spent inspiring, encouraging, connecting, training, and supporting individuals and groups as they consider, adopt, and adapt the Transition model, what has the Transition Movement as a whole managed to accomplish? Is it currently on track to deliver on its audacious intention to catalyze regeneration, not just a little in some places but a lot everywhere? While this level of influence and impact is almost too much to ask from any one movement, if it isn't what we're actually aiming for, we should at least be honest about that.

Since 2008, Transition US has officially recognized 175 Transition Initiatives across 39 states, and there are hundreds of other groups that have self-identified as part of the Transition Movement but never applied for official status. However, of those 175 official initiatives, 129 were recognized during just the first five years of Transition US, and as of 2022, only 55 remained active. Similarly, 120 of the 144 Transition Trainings that have taken place in the US happened prior to 2013.[3]

While Transition in the US is not necessarily representative of the Transition Movement as a whole, this seems to be part of a general pattern. When Transition first lands in a place, there's an initial burst of interest and excitement that tapers off after a few years. I believe there are several reasons for this: a chronic lack of capacity within Transition Hubs to provide the support local initiatives need, high levels of burnout and interpersonal conflict, and the sheer complexity inherent in Transition work.

I also believe unrealistic expectations may have played a role. In Richard Heinberg's foreword to *The Transition Handbook*, he described the Transition Movement as being "more like a party than a protest march."[4] Although this playful, optimistic tone, which has been characteristic of Transition from the beginning, clearly resonated with many people and likely helped spread the movement faster than it would have otherwise, it also failed to prepare Transition leaders for the scale of the challenges ahead. In retrospect, it's obvious that changing the world was never going to be easy, but many fell into the trap of thinking that Transition would be the exception. As it gradually became apparent that this work would take a lot longer and require a lot more effort than most initially expected, many simply gave up.

This problem is far from unique to Transition. Only about one-third of small businesses survive their first decade,[5] and I suspect that percentage is significantly higher for grassroots activist groups. In his 1987 "Movement Action Plan," veteran activist Bill Moyer wrote:

> Within a few years after achieving the goals of "take-off," every major social movement of the past twenty years has undergone a significant collapse, in which activists believed that their movements had failed, the power institutions were too powerful, and their own efforts were futile. This has happened even when movements were actually progressing reasonably well along the normal path taken by past successful movements![6]

Backing up his theory with examples from the US civil rights, anti-interventionist, and antinuclear movements, Moyer identified eight stages movements typically pass through on their way to widespread acceptance and transformation:

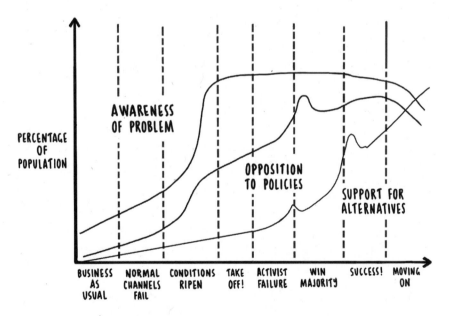

Figure 12.2: Bill Moyer's Movement Action Plan.

The most important thing to note here is that Take-Off, which is the stage in which a movement is growing fastest, is only stage four. While public awareness tends to plateau and drop off after that, support for the movement's aims continues to increase. If we quit in stage five because we incorrectly assume our movement has failed, we'll never achieve majority support or ultimate success. Even the most successful movements only have a short time in the spotlight, preceded and followed by hard work in relative obscurity.

This reminds me of a conversation I had at the 2018 Northern California Permaculture Convergence with the executive director of a buzzy new nonprofit I had often heard mentioned but had never met. A mutual friend introduced him to me (only half-jokingly) as "the most popular man in San Francisco." At one point, I asked him how Slow Money Northern California was doing, because his work was similarly focused on local investment. His response was deeply disappointing: "Who cares? Slow Money's only moving tens of millions of dollars. We need to be operating on a much bigger scale!" Although I told him I agreed with him about the need to continue to scale up, I also pressed him further about his assessment of Slow Money: "What other organization or movement is currently moving more money into local food businesses?" Unable to answer, he abruptly changed the subject.

I share this anecdote because I believe it's representative of how a lot of people feel about the Transition Movement these days. Whenever a bright new shiny movement comes along, a lot of people understandably get excited and stop whatever they're doing to jump on board. However, if we're constantly chasing after the next big thing, more established movements that have been quietly building power for decades will end up drained of their vitality. Instead of concluding that these movements have failed simply because they haven't fully succeeded yet, we could choose to double-down on their development.

Emerging Themes

In terms of the Five Stages of Transition, we could think of the Transition Movement's first decade as representing just its Starting Out phase. We tried a bunch of different things, brought together the Innovators and Early Adopters, and learned a lot about what works and what doesn't.

Beginning in 2017, I started to sense a shift into Deepening. This was the year Transition US hosted its first National Gathering and the international Hubs Group formed. Since that time (and apropos to the Deepening stage), more and more local organizers have been stepping up into regional, national, and international leadership roles, and there's been an increased focus on strengthening internal systems of governance.

Nevertheless, I believe we still have a lot more work to do in Deepening before we can open a door to Connecting and Building. Most Transition Hubs, including Transition Network, remain caught in a vicious cycle of limited capacity, limited impact, limited support, and limited resources. How might we reverse this pattern and unleash a "second wave" of Transition globally?

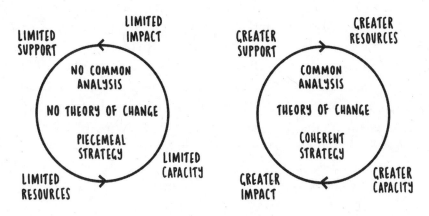

Figure 12.3: Vicious and virtuous cycles of organizational development.

I presented my analysis of the state of the Transition Movement in the previous section and proposed a theory of change in the form of the Five Stages of Transition. Now, I want to offer some thoughts about what might be an effective strategy for the Transition Movement moving forward. Because strategy helps us make the best use of the capacity we currently have, it's an important leverage point, especially when the resources we have are limited and the mission we aspire to fulfill is vast.

Supporting local initiatives: The complexity of the Transition Movement is both one of its greatest strengths and toughest challenges. While I would caution against oversimplifying the Transition approach, our main issue is that we usually try to do too much and end up spreading ourselves far too thin. Developing thriving Transition Initiatives all over the world is complex enough. We should trust other movements to handle their part.

While supporting Transition Initiatives has always been the explicit mandate of Transition Hubs, they haven't always acted like it. When I joined Transition US in 2017, one of the first things I noticed was that our relationships with initiatives throughout the country had atrophied to the point that we no longer even had current contact information for most of them. So much time had been spent simply trying to keep the organization afloat and working on side projects that it wasn't fulfilling its core purpose. This is a pattern I've observed at the international level as well.

Because the local level is where change really happens, I believe Transition Hubs should concentrate more on nurturing the health and vitality of Transition Initiatives as their niche and North Star. We can do this by staying in closer contact with local leaders and communicating with them more frequently about their needs and desires, by promoting more of their events and sharing more of their stories, and by developing a much more comprehensive training program that addresses every aspect of Transition. Whatever we do, I think we need to be asking ourselves: how will this help to strengthen initiatives at the local level? Is it providing local leaders with the knowledge, tools, skills, and resources they need to deepen, broaden, and scale up?

Shifting movement culture: The prevailing culture of the Transition Movement is another issue we need to confront. Although there are many wonderful things about how this movement has learned to work together and its efforts to encourage Inner Transition and Healthy Groups are commendable, I believe we still need to address issues around money, power, accountability, and professionalism. Our movement's aversion to money and power has kept most Transition Initiatives small and underresourced, while its aversion to accountability and professionalism has meant that disruptive and harmful behavior is too often tolerated.

If being fully enlightened was a prerequisite for engaging in Transition, none of us would qualify. Nevertheless, I think we need to at least ensure that those in leadership positions aren't actively harming the groups they're supposed to be serving. One way we might do this is by collaboratively creating a universal code of conduct for the movement that's based on the eight Transition Principles I described in chapter 4. This would apply to leaders at every level of the movement and include transparent and equitable processes to review and respond to complaints.

To help Transitioners overcome their resistance to dealing with issues of money and power, I believe we need to send a clear message that money and power aren't inherently bad. The way we use them can be shaped in accordance with our values, and embracing them is really the only way we'll be able to accomplish our aims. I think we also need to collect more best practices in both of these areas and disseminate them widely.

Prioritizing justice: Because of how it decentralizes wealth and power, seeks to include everyone, and practices deep democracy, I've always thought of Transition as a movement for justice as much as for sustainability. Nevertheless, we haven't always done a great job of communicating or embodying this. One of the biggest criticisms of the Transition Movement has long been its lack of diversity.[7] Despite many efforts over the years to partner with environmental justice groups, engage youth and frontline communities, and lift up leaders of color, Transition remains overwhelmingly made up of older (mostly white) people of privilege.

I believe there are two reasons for this. One is that Transition originally came from England, and its initial demographics have been self-reinforcing. When people don't see others who look like them, they may reasonably conclude that they aren't welcome or don't belong. We also need to do a better job of demonstrating that Transition has the ability to solve pressing problems for those currently in need. If you're simply struggling to pay your bills and raise your family, it's much more difficult to find the energy to care about issues that seem abstract and distant. In addition to preparing society as a whole for the Great Transition, we need to show how the tools this movement has developed can be used to strengthen the resilience of frontline communities right now.

It's also important that we continue to educate ourselves about issues related to positionality and privilege, and diversify leadership teams at all levels. However, we must be careful not to take the colonizing and tokenizing approach of trying to get more diverse people to join our cause merely because we don't want to appear racist. For the Transition Movement to become authentically diverse, we need to prioritize justice and incorporate it into everything we do.

Softening boundaries: While Transition regularly partners with many other movements, some of the language it uses gives outsiders the impression that it's a club with a secret handshake. By relying too much on insider jargon (such as the Great Reskilling and the Great Unleashing) and branding everything as Transition this or that, we have inadvertently created the appearance of a rigid boundary between what Transition is and isn't. This has undoubtedly alienated many people who might have otherwise become involved.

Although there is undeniable value to having a consistent, identifiable brand, much can be gained by softening our boundaries a bit. Sometimes even small tweaks can make a big difference. For example, trainings don't have to be called Transition Launch and Transition Thrive. The biggest training Transition US ever held was called Regenerative Leadership for Social Change, and our biggest conference was named the Regenerative Communities Summit.

I freely admit that I was initially a regeneration skeptic. When my colleague Mario Yanez suggested to me at the first annual Florida Permaculture Convergence in 2013 that "regeneration" would be the term to unite our related movements, I thought it was a little too New Agey to be widely embraced. However, over the past decade, I've gradually come to accept that regeneration actually describes what Transition is about better than words like "relocalization" and "resilience" we've used in the past. While still acknowledging the need for radical change, regeneration affirms our belief that a better world is still possible and that the work of Transition is fundamentally about protecting and enhancing life.

Dreaming bigger: If we're able to make these changes quickly enough, I believe we'll have a chance to unleash a second wave of Transition that's orders of magnitude bigger than its first. Up to this point, we've been ahead of the curve, but that won't always be the case. As the Great Unraveling continues apace, more and more people will begin seeking out positive, holistic, and practical alternatives to the status quo. This could lead to a massive surge of participation in movements like Transition, but only if we're ready to receive it.

One recurring dream I've had is for the Transition Movement to become a major partner for the Civilian Climate Corps that's been envisioned as part of the Green New Deal.[8] Transition Initiatives could provide the knowledge, skills, and people power to organize educational campaigns, facilitate community dialogues, retrofit millions of homes and buildings for energy efficiency, set up composting hubs and food forests in urban neighborhoods, and install edible gardens and rainwater harvesting systems.

Transition could also play a major role in shaping the largest transfer of generational wealth in human history, which is just beginning to flow from Baby Boomer parents to their Gen X and Millennial kids. Because younger people tend to be a lot more progressive, if we can show them a movement truly worth investing in, we could see a dramatic increase in funding for our initiatives. We need to think bigger like this, but unless we do the hard work of Deepening and Connecting first, Building and Daring to Dream as a movement will remain just a fantasy.

A Movement of Movements

While I've used Transition as an extended case study throughout this book, it's far from the only movement that matters. In his keynote for the 2007 Bioneers conference, Paul Hawken estimated there were at least 130,000 groups at that time working for social and environmental justice around the world.[9] That same year, he and his team launched a website called WiserEarth to connect all these groups. Before it was decommissioned in 2014 due to rising upkeep costs, WiserEarth cataloged over 114,000 groups.[10]

I can't help but think that maybe this was for the best. Our global movement of movements should be much too big to fit under even the biggest umbrella. What's most important isn't building the perfect platform and trying to get everybody to adopt it but simply acknowledging and appreciating that we're already part of something much greater than ourselves.

I've come to envision this movement of movements as an ancient tree that's deeply rooted in the wisdom of the Earth and whose massive trunk represents the Indigenous cultures of the world. Its branches represent the various movements that exist in our world today, and its leaves symbolize the groups that are part of them. Some movements are more closely related than others, but we're all part of one family.

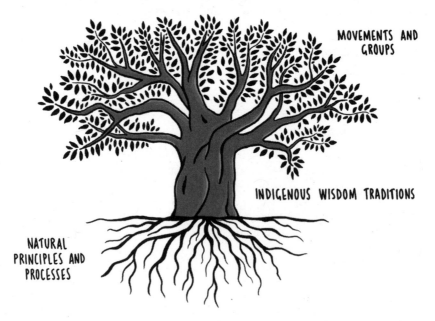

Figure 12.4: The movement of movements.

Beyond simply acknowledging and celebrating this movement of movements, we should also try to at least support and work together with those that are most closely related to our own. We can do this by sharing information about each other; collaborating on events, projects, and campaigns; and forming ongoing partnerships and coalitions. For example, because of the close complementary relationship between Transition and Permaculture, I frequently encourage Transitioners to take a Permaculture Design Course, practice Permaculture in their daily lives, and incorporate its principles into their work.

Below are some of my favorite organizations and movements that are part of just one movement cluster we might call the "regenerative communities movement." Some are entities I have worked extensively with, while others I have merely admired from afar.

Context and vision: Promoting a better understanding of the issues we're currently facing as well as their most promising solutions is essential for ensuring that a wiser and more compassionate society emerges from the Great Unraveling. For more than two decades, Post Carbon Institute has been a leader in this area, sharing valuable perspectives and analysis through numerous books, reports, podcasts, and videos, as well as their Resilience.org website.[11] I'm honored to also be part of the Great Transition Network, a collection of over a thousand leading academics and activists from all over the world who exchange essays on a monthly basis, exploring questions like "What fresh lessons, insight, and inspiration can we glean from a long view of history?" and "How might we catalyze a global citizens movement?"

Inner Transition: Some of my favorite organizations focusing on the Inner Transition include the Deep Adaptation Forum, which supports people grappling with the possibility of civilizational collapse; the Work That Reconnects Network, which features facilitators from all over the world dedicated to disseminating the teachings and practices of Joanna Macy; and the Animas Valley Institute, a Colorado-based nonprofit that organizes wilderness expeditions for participants seeking to connect with their deepest nature.

Healthy groups: As previously mentioned, most of what I know about working in collaborative groups I've learned from living in intentional communities and working with Nick Osborne of Evolving Organisation. However, I've also learned a lot from the Center for Nonviolent Communication, Sociocracy for All, Holacracy, ProSocial World, and the Right Use of Power Institute. The Art of Hosting is notable for teaching a wide variety of techniques for large group facilitation, including Appreciative Inquiry, World Cafe, and Open Space Technology.

Local food systems: So many inspiring efforts are happening in this area that it's hard to even know where to begin. There's the self-described "international peasants' movement" known as La Via Campesina, the Afro-Indigenous food justice organization Soul Fire Farm, and the National Young Farmers Coalition. The Slow Food Movement, which started in Italy in the 1980s as a response to a McDonald's opening beside the Spanish Steps in Rome, has since spread to 1,600 communities in 160 countries and seeded other movements like Slow Money. The Permaculture Movement remains highly decentralized but is supported by various international, national, and regional organizations such as the Permaculture Research Institute, the Permaculture Institute of North America, and the Permaculture Association of the Northeast.

Solidarity economies: The term "solidarity economy" is used worldwide to link together many different kinds of initiatives that are building more cooperative, just, and sustainable economies. Here in the US, the largest solidarity economy network is the New Economy Coalition, which supports more than 200 member organizations. They include Shareable, which promotes sharing economy solutions through its publications, podcasts, and how-to guides; the Sustainable Economies Law Center, which provides legal advice for progressive community-based organizations; and Resource Generation, which encourages young people with class privilege to redistribute their wealth to social justice causes.

Climate justice: The mother of all climate justice organizations is still 350. org, which Bill McKibben created with a group of Middlebury College students in 2008. However, in recent years, McKibben has moved on to working with elder activists through his new organization, Third Act, while other youth-led movements have stepped to the fore. They include Greta Thunberg's Fridays for the Future, but also the Sunrise Movement, Power Shift, Zero Hour, Just Stop Oil, and Last Generation. Extinction Rebellion will always have a special place in my heart for how it enlivens its provocative actions with ample art and humor.

Intentional communities: The intentional communities movement includes co-ops, where residents tend to live together under one roof, as well as cohousing developments and ecovillages, where members share common spaces and other amenities but typically have their own houses. Two organizations supporting intentional communities worldwide are the Foundation for Intentional Community and the Global Ecovillage Network. Each offers a directory of communities, educational programs and resources, and support for communities in crisis. Through my involvement with the Boulder Housing Coalition, I've also been part of the North American Students of Cooperation, which supports 50 (student and nonstudent) co-ops throughout the US.

Other related movements: In addition to the previously mentioned organizations and movements, there are many others that don't fit neatly into any of the categories above. A few of my favorite misfits are the Permaculture Action Network, which partners with well-known artists like Michael Franti and Rising Appalachia to promote Permaculture Action Days; the City Repair Project, a long-time leader in the field of creative placemaking; and Ecosystem Restoration Communities, a global network of grassroots efforts working to regenerate degraded ecologies. Other organizations seek to weave together all the strands of the regenerative communities movement, such as the Thriving Resilient Communities Collaboratory in the US, ECOLISE in Europe, and the Global Tapestry of Alternatives internationally.

Conclusion

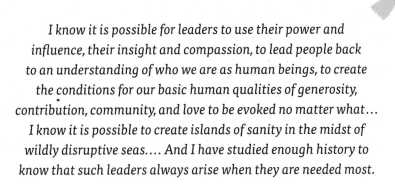

I know it is possible for leaders to use their power and influence, their insight and compassion, to lead people back to an understanding of who we are as human beings, to create the conditions for our basic human qualities of generosity, contribution, community, and love to be evoked no matter what… I know it is possible to create islands of sanity in the midst of wildly disruptive seas…. And I have studied enough history to know that such leaders always arise when they are needed most.

— Margaret Wheatley, *Who Do We Choose to Be?*[1]

If we're going to do what it takes to actually save our world, we need an unshakeable conviction that it's worth saving. I occasionally hear from people (including some who are generally well-meaning and intelligent) that nothing we do could possibly matter in the grand scheme of things, so why bother? Everything ends, all species eventually die, and Earth would probably be better off without us. I suspect a lot of us secretly hold these kinds of beliefs to some extent.

While understandable, this logic is based on several fundamental misperceptions about the nature of reality. Life is not purely chaotic and meaningless, nor is humanity beyond redemption. In fact, there is ample evidence to suggest that we are miraculous beings on an extraordinary planet in the midst of a vast, sacred universe. Though detachment promises transcendent peace, it never delivers. Deep down, we know everything is interconnected, and ultimately, we can't fool ourselves.

In his 2011 documentary, *Journey of the Universe*, evolutionary cosmologist Brian Swimme explains that if the rate of our universe's expansion was just one millionth of one percent faster, it would have flung its primordial matter so far apart that galaxies and planets wouldn't have formed. Similarly, if our universe had expanded even one millionth of one percent more slowly, everything would have collapsed into a black hole, ending the potential for life as we know it. Swimme sums up the meaning of this by saying, "What we've discovered is that we're living in a universe that is expanding at exactly the rate necessary for life and structure to come forth. It could be, then, that even though we can't call the early universe 'alive,' we can understand it as 'life-generating.'"[2]

NASA scientist James Lovelock expressed a similar idea in his 1979 book, *Gaia: A New Look at Life on Earth*.[3] Although his "Gaia hypothesis," which describes our planet as a self-regulating superorganism, was initially ridiculed, it has become increasingly accepted by the scientific community. Key evidence supporting it includes the consistency of global temperature, atmospheric composition, and ocean salinity throughout Earth's history. Since life began, global temperature has remained remarkably constant, even though the amount of heat radiating from the sun has increased by about 25 percent, and despite salt being continually washed from land into the oceans, salinity has hovered around 4 percent for billions of years. This is partly thanks to tiny creatures called coccolithophores that capture excess salt in their shells and deposit it into the ocean floor when they die.

Although it boggles the mind to try to understand how trillions of individual organisms could cooperate to achieve such a mutually beneficial state, our own bodies are made up of trillions of individual cells that work together every minute of every day to maintain an optimal balance. While we may never fully comprehend how life works, it undeniably does. It intrinsically knows how to enable more and more life to thrive, and human beings have this same regenerative potential.

Technology continues to progress, but we're still far from being able to create anything as complex, intelligent, and beautiful as an earthworm, let alone a tree, a butterfly, or a human being. Standing on the leading edge of 14 billion years of cosmic evolution and 3.5 billion years of the evolution of life here on Earth, if we pause for even a moment to consider how much struggle and sacrifice it took for our ancestors to get us here, it's impossible to believe that throwing all of that away is no big deal.

While we might envision a sci-fi future where we leave a ruined Earth behind to hop around from one galaxy to the next, we should check the math on this. The closest potentially habitable planet to Earth is currently thought to be Proxima Centauri b. Even at the fastest speed ever recorded for manned spacecraft, it would take a person nearly 114,000 years to travel there.[4] For practical purposes, we should consider ourselves here for the duration. Earth really is our only home. There's no Planet B.

The good news is that Earth will survive whatever we throw at it, and it's highly unlikely that humanity will go extinct in the near future. What's much more likely, if we fail to act, is that billions will suffer and die, and the range of possibilities available to subsequent generations will be greatly diminished. This is why we must rise to the challenges of our times.

We can't simply tune out our world, telling ourselves that someone else will handle it. If we excuse ourselves from taking action because others aren't acting either, nobody will step up and our world will gradually become smaller and more dangerous. However, if we can find the courage to lean into this Great Transition, our bravery will inspire others to do the same.

We might even consider that the journey humanity has been on for the past 10,000 years has been a necessary stage in our overall evolution. We could imagine our species as an unruly teenager who has rebelled against its parents to test boundaries, differentiate itself, and figure out

Table 13.1. Beliefs inspiring apathy and action

The Dominant Paradigm	Evolutionary Change
Reality is chaotic and meaningless	Reality is miraculous and intelligent
Life is disposable	Life is sacred
Humanity is inherently destructive	Humanity shares nature's capacity for regeneration
It doesn't matter what I do	Everything we do makes a difference
We're already doomed	Our story is still being written

who it really is. Now, having run up against global limits for the first time, we might finally be ready to enter into species adulthood with its many responsibilities, but also its wisdom, dignity, and power. In this way, the Great Unraveling could serve as an initiatory ordeal for humanity.

In many traditional societies, rites of passage mark the transition from adolescence to adulthood. Sometimes, these trials are extremely intense, and not everybody makes it back alive. As frightening as this is, it seems to me a more helpful way to look at our current predicament than as some kind of cosmic mistake or proof that humanity is fatally flawed.

Although we can and should condemn the many atrocities that have transpired during this time, it's also essential that we appreciate the many advances modern civilization has brought about. From the ability to connect with people all over the world and access vast stores of knowledge with just the push of a button to increased life expectancy and material comfort, we should work to preserve these things as much as possible even as we seek to abandon many other harmful trappings of modernity.

We need to combine the best of the past with the best of the present to bring about a regenerative future. Eight billion people simply cannot return to being hunter-gatherers. For the first time ever, humanity is faced with having to consciously create a just and sustainable global culture.

However, this unique challenge also presents a unique opportunity for us to awaken and realize our unfulfilled potential. I would even go so far as to say that I believe we can't be truly happy or whole at this time in history unless we are involved somehow in helping to heal our world.

Take just a moment to envision what humanity might achieve in the future if we're able to cross this evolutionary threshold. Our sun isn't expected to boil Earth's seas for another one to two billion years. How might we continue to evolve if we can find a way now to live in harmony with nature? It's possible that this existential crisis could draw out of us qualities we've never before imagined. As Swimme poetically observes: "The planet earth was once molten rock and now sings operas."

This is what I come back to when all other hope is lost: an appreciation of the sacredness of existence and my responsibility to uphold and embody it as best I can. We all have this potential. It's in our DNA, embedded in the fundamental patterns of our universe. Like it or not, we are all protagonists in a story that will be remembered for generations to come. What do we want those who come after us to say about us, perhaps sitting around the fire in the ruins of the postindustrial age? That we sat by and watched the Great Unraveling unfold on the evening news or that we did everything we possibly could, just as soon as we knew?

How Life Could Win

In March 2020, just as the coronavirus lockdowns were starting here in the US, Rob Hopkins published a new post to his blog titled "What did Sisyphus dream of?" In it, he retells the Greek myth of a man condemned to push a boulder uphill forever and connects it to how many activists feel about working for a better world. We push and push, only to have our hopes tumble back down to the bottom and be forced to begin again. However, as he did so brilliantly before with the story of peak oil, here Hopkins flips another well-known story on its head:

> How would it feel to be on the other side of the hill, doing the work we do in a context where gravity is our friend? In a context where policy-making, and finance, and cultural norms are behind what we do, not in opposition to it? It would feel like a very different world, where policy and funding come to be in service of the rapid transition, where culture and stories of what's "normal" rapidly change, where the social permission for flying and other high carbon behaviours rapidly shift. From our position on this uphill side of the slope, it's hard to imagine it, but imagine it we must.[5]

Although we clearly haven't reached the other side yet, something eventually has to give. It's said all revolutions seem impossible until they happen. From 9/11 to the Great Recession to the election of Donald Trump to the COVID-19 pandemic, major world events continue to confound our expectations. We are shocked when black swans appear on a lake, but black swans have always existed.

I'm convinced that historic change will occur within my lifetime, but exactly how soon it will come and whether it will be positive or negative on the whole, I'm less certain. What we do in the coming years and decades will have a significant impact on its trajectory. As the Great Unraveling continues, the need for radical change will become more and more apparent, causing more and more people to seek out alternatives. At that point, the winds of change will be blowing at our backs. Our job as leaders is not primarily to create this wind but to be ready to harness it when it comes.

So, what are the most important actions we can take to steer humanity towards a regenerative future? As neoliberal economist Milton Friedman famously wrote: "When that crisis occurs, the actions that are taken depend on the ideas that are lying around. That, I believe, is our basic function: to develop alternatives to existing policies, to keep them alive and available until the politically impossible becomes the politically inevitable."[6] While I shudder to think what the late "shock doctor" would prescribe for our current predicament, he happens to be right in this one instance. In times of turmoil, which path is chosen depends on two main factors. I call them "the Two Imperatives."

1. We need to make the regenerative vision universally known: To accomplish this, we must do everything in our power to familiarize as many people as possible as soon as possible with concepts like the limits to growth, energy descent, relocalization, Permaculture, and Transition Towns. The more people have an accurate understanding of the root causes of the Great Unraveling and are aware of regenerative solutions, the less likely we will be to demonize and scapegoat each other when times get even tougher than they are now.

At the moment, these ideas are mostly unknown beyond a relatively small subculture of activists and other cultural creatives, but they need to be front and center in every discussion about our collective future. People need to be having conversations about them at coffee shops, churches, workplaces, and kitchen tables. The mainstream media needs to spend a lot more time covering the regenerative communities movement, and politicians need to be pressed about their plans for the Great Transition on debate stages.

Humanity always needs a guiding story, a better future to reach for. We can't help it. We tell ourselves stories to make sense of our lives and our world. They provide us with reference points and a sense of direction, offering us meaning and purpose.

For the past century, humanity's dominant story has been the American Dream of upward mobility and middle-class prosperity for everyone, two-and-a-half kids, and a white picket fence. While this isn't necessarily a bad vision, it's always been a lie. It's fundamentally unsustainable and has always been built on the backs of someone else: slaves, immigrants, women, the natural world, and future generations. Although it originated here in the US, the American Dream has since been exported around the globe, both by persuasion and by force.

Thomas Kuhn wrote that paradigm shifts occur when a previously established model is found to no longer adequately explain new realities.[7] In that space of uncertainty, new theories can be proposed and experimented with. Those that fit best with the totality of our knowledge and most accurately predict the future are adopted, while those that don't are eventually cast aside. I believe Charles Darwin said something similar.

This is exactly what's happening in our times. With each passing year, it's becoming clearer and clearer that the paradigm of the Industrial Growth Society is a threat to our very survival. Old certainties are breaking apart faster than ever before, which is hugely destabilizing but also has the potential to unlock previously unthinkable possibilities. There's even a chance that by having all of our conventional reference points stripped away, we might find our way back to what matters most.

As a candidate for the next American Dream, the regenerative vision has a lot going for it. It's compelling not only because of how it joins optimism with practicality but also because it honors who we fundamentally are as people. The overwhelming speed, complexity, abstraction, and isolation of modern life hasn't been making us happier. It's been making us sick. The regenerative vision points to a familiar but largely forgotten way of life that could be slower, simpler, and more satisfying, lived in closer connection with self, family, community, and nature.

2. We need to develop successful practical alternatives to the status quo in as many places as possible: Because regeneration runs so counter to the logic of the Industrial Growth Society, we not only need to "develop alternatives to existing policies," but also prototype living examples of the future we want. Practical projects, like those mentioned in chapter 11, enable people to experience for themselves how abstract concepts like degrowth, mutual aid, and community resilience manifest in the real world and help them to trust that they're nothing to fear.

We need to recognize how big an ask Transition actually is. We're asking people to take all of their eggs out of the basket of the Industrial Growth Society and place them in our basket. If you've kept all of your eggs in the basket of the Industrial Growth Society your entire life without any of them breaking, you might be a little skeptical when a stranger walks up to you and says: "Why don't you take all your eggs out of that basket and put them in ours?" You might want to take a long, hard look at that basket first. Is it frayed or full of holes? Will my eggs end up splattered all over the pavement?

To convince people that our basket is big and sturdy enough, we need to prove that our ideas can work, not just a little in a few places, but a lot everywhere. We need to prove that regenerative solutions can put money in people's pockets, food on their tables, and roofs over their heads. We also need to prove that people will be happier living this way.

However, if this movement of movements can start making changes for the better at scale, people will notice. In contrast to all the bad news we're bombarded with daily, something like this could really stand out. Eventually, we might even be able to show a clear contrast between communities who are actively transitioning and thriving as a result and those that are failing because they're trying to hang on to the past.

These are the two big things I believe we need to do to give ourselves a chance of winning the future, for ourselves and for all life. While it's almost inconceivable right now that regeneration could become the dominant paradigm guiding the future of humanity, if we can fulfill these Two Imperatives far enough in advance of global systems collapse, we can shift the Overton Window. Unfamiliar and unproven ideas often appear radical at first, but can gradually become perceived as more and more acceptable, sensible, and popular over time. Some previously unthinkable ideas may even end up becoming our new normal.

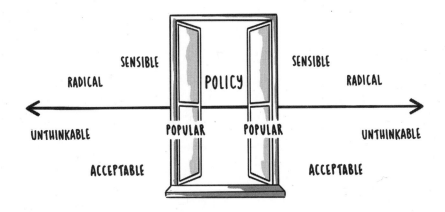

Figure 13.2: The Overton Window.

Even if we're able to accomplish this, however, there will still be many challenges ahead for humanity. There will undoubtedly be opposition to these changes and fierce debates about how best to reconfigure society. Also, no matter what we do now, the effects of climate change will be with us for a long time, and we can expect unforeseen issues to crop up as well. We'll inevitably make mistakes and need to keep iterating in order to arrive at a relatively stable state.

Nevertheless, the sooner we commit to a path of evolutionary change and regeneration, the more time we'll have to rebuild community connections and put in place alternative systems. The more awareness we're able to raise, the more food we're able to grow, and the more renewable energy we're able to bring online before things go completely sideways, the better off we'll be. This might end up making the difference between a just transition or a future controlled by the disaster capitalists. If we focus on fulfilling these Two Imperatives now, we'll all have a much better chance to shape our own destiny.

Going Forth

The first stage in the Spiral of the Work That Reconnects, Coming from Gratitude, encourages us to begin our journey by rooting ourselves in profound appreciation for all that life has given us. Even if our lives have been difficult, we can be grateful that we're still here and that every moment offers new opportunities for transformation. This enables us to move into the second stage, Honoring Our Pain for the World, without becoming overwhelmed. While most of us usually try to ignore and push aside our feelings of grief, anger, fear, and hopelessness, acknowledging and embracing them opens up possibilities for Seeing with New Eyes. Then, with a fresh perspective and a renewed sense of purpose, inspiration can guide our actions Going Forth.

Figure 13.3: The Spiral of the Work That Reconnects,
plotted against a U shape.

Although I haven't presented these stages in an entirely linear way, this is essentially the journey we've been on for the past twelve and a half chapters. We've contemplated the beauty and sacredness of life, confronted the complexity and urgency of our global polycrisis, and explored many different ways we can help bring about a better future. Now, as we're approaching the end of our time here together, it's time to think about next steps.

In doing so, I'd like to caution you not to try to change everything at once. This will inevitably leave you feeling overwhelmed and spread too thin to really change anything. Instead, we should always be guided by what feels like the natural next step on our path, what's sometimes called the "adjacent possible."

As long as we do that, it doesn't really matter where we begin. Growing a garden or engaging in activism can lead to an interest in mindfulness (and vice versa). What is most important is to not hesitate. Whatever is calling to us at this very moment, we should do it. Avoid the trap of analysis paralysis.

One thing you could do is to revisit chapters of this book you'd like to study in greater depth. I think most people have had the experience of reading a book more than once and discovering new insights each time. In the process of writing *The Regeneration Handbook*, I condensed more than 1,000 pages of material into the comparatively slim volume you hold in your hands. Because this content has been so highly concentrated, rereadings will likely prove especially fruitful.

If you're currently part of a changemaking group, you might consider sharing with them what you've learned and propose studying this book together. You might also investigate the dozens of books, films, reports, and articles in my bibliography and endnotes. Although I've mentioned most only in passing, each is a veritable treasure trove of valuable perspectives and practices just waiting to be broken open. Engaging with them will lead you to additional resources.

As important as it is, developing our intellectual understanding of regeneration and evolutionary change is really only a first step. We eventually need to move beyond Preparation into Action. This might involve establishing an ongoing practice of self-transformation, working to make your household as sustainable and resilient as possible, or volunteering with an organization that inspires you.

For those interested in getting involved in the Transition Movement, I encourage you to visit Transition Network's website and check whether there's already a local initiative near you. If not, you could sign up for a

Transition Training and consider whether you might want to start a new group. You could even organize a training in your local community to kick-start this process.

I've often been asked by people from progressive hot spots like Portland, Oregon, Asheville, North Carolina, and Madison, Wisconsin, that already have many similar groups whether they should start a Transition Initiative. Of course, not every town needs one, but I do think most communities would benefit from having something like it: a group with a holistic vision for the future that's inclusive and collaborative, able to complement existing efforts and weave them together into a powerful movement.

Beyond Transition, many other excellent organizations and movements could use your support. I featured a few of my favorites in the previous chapter, but the best way to find a group you might want to get involved with is simply to ask for suggestions from trusted sources in your local community, attend some of their events, and start making connections.

It's also possible you might feel that you're ready to launch your own nonprofit or regenerative business. While creating one from scratch can be enormously challenging, I certainly wouldn't want to discourage anyone from trying. Our world needs more people daring enough to venture into uncharted territories and blaze new trails.

When I was at Naropa, I remember reading a photocopied magazine article of an interview with the Dalai Lama. Although I can no longer find it, as best I can recall, he was saying that the biggest problem with environmentalists is we aren't sufficiently confident in our convictions. We have the right vision but tend to be much too timid in pursuing it. William Butler Yeats similarly lamented that "The best lack all conviction, while the worst / Are full of passionate intensity."[8] We should be at least as confident as they are and give ourselves permission to be passionately intense about our lives and our potential; about learning, growing, and evolving; about justice and regeneration; and about manifesting the more creative, cooperative, joyful, and loving world we envision.

To help you create your plan for Going Forth, I've adapted an exercise from the Work That Reconnects called "Goals and Resources."[9] This activity is typically done in pairs, with one person asking questions and writing down answers while the other person responds. Although it's helpful to have someone else to witness and hold us accountable to our aspirations, if you don't happen to have that person at the moment, you could simply journal on each of the following questions by yourself.

1. If you could do anything, what would you do right now for the healing of our world? If you've completed the Discovering Purpose exercise from chapter 8, you could use your Ikigai as a starting point. Then, reflect further on what living into your "reason for being" might actually look like and involve. While you probably won't be able to completely realize your vision by next week or the week after, that isn't a problem. This activity is merely a way to get started.

2. What resources do you have, inner and outer, that will help you accomplish this? Chances are, you don't realize yet how much relevant knowledge, skills, and support you already have. Take whatever time is required to list all of the tangible and intangible resources you can currently access and think about how you might call on them when they're needed.

3. What resources, inner and outer, will you need to acquire? If you've picked a goal that's ambitious enough, it's likely you don't have all of necessary resources yet. What capacities and connections can you start cultivating now in order to create the conditions for change to occur?

4. What obstacles, inner and outer, might you encounter? Although we can't fully anticipate what might happen along our path, it makes sense to prepare for obvious pitfalls. It's also worth considering how we might self-sabotage. Are there patterns we've observed in ourselves in the past that might keep us from achieving our goals?

5. How might you overcome these obstacles? Here's an opportunity to sketch out strategies for addressing the internal and external challenges you just identified. Often, if we're able to overcome our self-imposed obstacles, overcoming our external obstacles seems easy in comparison.

6. What can you do in the next few weeks to get started? This last question effectively calls our bluff by asking us to commit to a specific action. Do we really want to do this or not? If we do, we should be able to figure out at least one action we can take in the next few weeks to begin. Even a small gesture can greatly strengthen our resolve and enable us to feel our calling starting to come into existence.

This exercise can be repeated whenever we're feeling uncertain about what to do next. Like most patterns of Transformation, we don't just cycle through the Spiral of the Work once. Instead, we pass through its stages again and again, deepening our understanding, broadening our vision, and scaling up our action with every revolution.

The Theory of Anyway

In 2007, homesteader and prolific blogger Sharon Astyk published a short but powerful piece about an idea a friend of hers called "the Theory of Anyway."[10] By this, her friend meant that even if our world wasn't in the midst of an unprecedented crisis, she would still choose to live in a regenerative way and work for a regenerative future, simply because that's how she prefers to live and because it's the right thing to do.

This reminds me of one of my favorite satirical cartoons. Maybe you've seen it.[11] It's of a guy in a suit and tie, standing at a podium at a big climate summit, gesturing up at a series of bullet points displayed on a screen above him. They're touting some of the many benefits of climate action: "Energy Independence," "Preserve Rainforests," "Green Jobs," "Liveable Cities," "Clean Water, Air," and "Healthy Children." Aghast, someone in the audience stands up and shouts: "What if it's a big hoax and we create a better world for nothing?"

Unfortunately, we are in the midst of an unprecedented global crisis, and climate change is most definitely not a hoax, but even if this wasn't the case, we could still find plenty of reasons to engage in this work. I know I would, simply because it's the best thing I'm able to imagine. I find this work to be endlessly fascinating and immensely rewarding. It's stretched me in ways I didn't even know were possible and has undoubtedly made me a better person. I've met many of the most extraordinary people I know through this work, and the life it's opened up for me has already led beyond my wildest dreams.

Whether we're a parent, a teacher, an engineer, an artist, a designer, a builder, a healer, a farmer, an entrepreneur, or an activist, we all have our own evolutionary journey to make. Whatever our circumstances and predispositions, we all have the ability to help bring a little more light into this world and leave behind a legacy we can be proud of.

Sometimes, when I'm feeling particularly down about the state of our world, I ask myself: even if all of the worst-case (or best-case) scenarios were confirmed, would I want to be doing anything different? Repeatedly calling my bluff like this has led me to realize that my genuine motivation in working for a Great Transition is less about trying to prevent catastrophe (though that would be nice) than it is about heeding my own calling and wanting to help others do the same.

Regardless of the outcome, I want to know that I've tried my best. I want to help bring as much beauty as I possibly can into this world and die without regrets. I know I can't do everything, but if I turn away from what's mine to do, I won't be able to live with myself and depression will eventually overtake me. I also know that when I'm my most authentic self, serving a greater purpose, it's as if the entire cosmos is rooting me on.

The only real antidote to feelings of powerlessness lies in banding together and taking action. The cavalry isn't coming, and we are the ones we've been waiting for.[12] We should never forget this awesome power that lives within us, never forget the patterns of evolutionary change are in our favor, and never give up on ourselves. Evolution is constantly unfurling itself, within us and beyond.

May this *Regeneration Handbook* be of benefit to countless sentient beings throughout space and time and help to bring about a future that is truly just and regenerative. As water cuts the deepest canyon and light dispels the darkness, may we be a rushing river and a torch. May we forever be rooted in the abundant generosity of the Earth and aspire to the expansiveness of our sky.

Notes

Chapter 1: Introduction

1. *Cosmos*, hosted by Carl Sagan (United States: Public Broadcasting Service, 1980).
2. "The Arc of the Moral Universe Is Long, But It Bends Toward Justice," *Quote Investigator*, November 15, 2012.
3. This term was coined by Kenneth Boulding in his 1965 book, *The Meaning of the 20th Century: The Great Transition*. Ecophilosopher Joanna Macy and author David Korten use a similar term: "the Great Turning."
4. "Country Trends: United States of America: Ecological Footprint (Number of Earths)," Global Footprint Network, accessed September 4, 2023.
5. Andrew King, "Global Warming Is Likely to Breach the 1.5-Degree-C Milestone within 5 Years," *Scientific American*, May 17, 2023.

Chapter 2: Patterns of Evolution

1. Christopher Alexander, Sara Ishikawa, and Murray Silverstein, with Max Jacobson, Ingrid Fiksdahl-King, and Shlomo Angel, *A Pattern Language: Towns, Buildings, Construction* (New York: Oxford University Press, 1977), xli.
2. If you'd like to join me in geeking out on these topics, I'd suggest Fritjof Capra, *The Web of Life: A New Scientific Understanding of Living Systems* (New York: Anchor Books, 1997) and Margaret Wheatley, *Leadership and the New Science: Discovering Order in a Chaotic World* (San Francisco: Berrett-Koehler, 2006).
3. Peter Senge, C. Otto Scharmer, Joseph Jaworski, and Betty Sue Flowers, *Presence: An Exploration of Profound Change in People, Organizations, and Society* (New York: Doubleday, 2005).
4. C. Otto Scharmer, *Theory U: Leading from the Future as It Emerges* (San Francisco: Berrett-Koehler, 2009).
5. Joseph Campbell, *The Hero with a Thousand Faces* (New York: Bollingen Foundation, 1949).
6. Toby Hemenway, *Gaia's Garden: A Guide to Home-Scale Permaculture* (White River Junction, VT: Chelsea Green, 2000), 19-20.
7. I learned this distinction between vertical and horizontal change from Buddhist teacher Reggie Ray and Bill Plotkin, *Wild Mind: A Field Guide to the Human Psyche* (Novato, CA: New World Library, 2013).

8. For more about the Five Buddha families, see Irini Rockwell, "The Five Buddha Families," *Lion's Roar*, September 5, 2018.

Chapter 3: My Evolutionary Journey

1. Bob Dylan, "It's Alright, Ma (I'm Only Bleeding)," track 10 on *Bringing It All Back Home*, Columbia Records, 1965.
2. M. K. Gandhi, *An Autobiography or the Story of My Experiments with Truth*, trans. Mahadev Desai (India: Navajivan Publishing House, 1968).
3. C. Otto Scharmer, *Theory U: Leading from the Future as It Emerges* (San Francisco: Berrett-Koehler, 2009), 119.
4. Ibid., 131.
5. Ibid., 143.
6. Ibid., 163.
7. Ibid., 191–192.
8. Post Carbon Institute's Relocalization Network was a direct precursor to the Transition Movement in the US. When Transition US formed in 2009, PCI generously provided seed funding and transferred its entire network to TUS.
9. Scharmer, *Theory U*, 203.
10. Ibid, 215.
11. Steve McAllister and Don Hall, *10 Stories of Transition in the US: Inspiring Examples of Community Resilience-Building* (Sebastopol, CA: Transition US, 2019).

Chapter 4: The Transition Story

1. This used to be posted prominently on Transition Network's website, but I can now only find a few different versions on other websites scattered throughout the internet.
2. Rob Hopkins, *The Transition Handbook: From Oil Dependency to Local Resilience* (England: Green Books, 2008), 135.
3. Joanna Macy and Molly Young Brown, *Coming Back to Life: Practices to Reconnect Our Lives, Our World* (Gabriola Island, BC: New Society, 1998), 17.
4. Craig K. Comstock, "The 'Transition Towns' Movement's Initial Genius," *Huffington Post*, November 27, 2010.
5. Hopkins, *The Transition Handbook*, 12.
6. *The End of Suburbia*, directed by Gregory Greene (Canada: The Electric Wallpaper Co, 2004).
7. The Students of Kinsale Further Education College and Rob Hopkins, *Kinsale 2021: An Energy Descent Action Plan* (Ireland: Kinsale Further Education College, 2005).
8. Hopkins, *The Transition Handbook*, 136–141.

9. Transition Town Totnes with Jacqui Hodgson and Rob Hopkins. *Transition in Action: Totnes and District 2030, An Energy Descent Action Plan* (England: Green Books, 2010).

10. Global map of Transition Initiatives, Hubs, and Trainers available at transitiongroups.org.

11. Hopkins, *The Transition Handbook*, 148.

12. Rob Hopkins, "Introducing a New Way of Understanding Transition," in *2010 Transition Network Conference Guide* (England: Transition Network, 2010), 6.

13. Rob Hopkins, *The Transition Companion: Making Your Community More Resilient in Uncertain Times* (White River Junction, VT: Chelsea Green, 2011).

14. Transition Network, *The Essential Guide to Doing Transition: Getting Transition Started in Your Street, Community, Town, or Organization* (England: Transition Network, 2016).

Chapter 5: The Five Stages of Transition

1. Rob Hopkins, *The Transition Companion: Making Your Community More Resilient in Uncertain Times* (White River Junction, VT: Chelsea Green, 2011), 15.

2. Ibid., 91.

3. Ibid., 143.

4. Henry D. Thoreau, *Walden; or, Life in the Woods* (Boston: Ticknor and Fields, 1854).

5. Hopkins, *The Transition Companion*, 197.

6. Ken Meter, *Sarasota County, Florida: Local Farm & Food Economy* (Minneapolis, MN: Crossroads Resource Center, 2006).

7. Hopkins, *The Transition Companion*, 234.

8. Ibid., 280.

Chapter 6: Our Global Context

1. James Joyce, *Ulysses* (Paris: Shakespeare and Company, 1922).

2. James Howard Kunstler, *The Long Emergency: Surviving the End of Oil, Climate Change, and Other Converging Catastrophes of the Twenty-First Century* (New York: Grove Press, 2006).

3. Richard Heinberg, *Peak Everything: Waking Up to the Century of Declines* (Gabriola Island, BC: New Society, 2010).

4. Movement Generation Justice & Ecology Project, *From Banks and Tanks to Cooperation and Caring: A Strategic Framework for a Just Transition* (Berkeley, CA: Movement Generation Justice & Ecology Project, 2017).

5. Donella H. Meadows, Dennis L. Meadows, Jørgen Randers, and William W. Behrens III, *The Limits to Growth: A Report for the Club of Rome's Project on the Predicament of Mankind* (United States: Potomac Associates, 1972).

6. Matt Simon, "The Infamous 1972 Report That Warned of Civilization's Collapse," *Wired*, July 6, 2022.

7. *Arithmetic, Population and Energy: Sustainability 101*, presented by Al Bartlett (Boulder, CO: University of Colorado, 2002). Bartlett gave this same talk 1,742 times throughout his life.

8. International Energy Agency, *World Energy Outlook 2010* (Paris: International Energy Agency, 2010).

9. Bill McKibben, "Global Warming's Terrifying New Math," *Rolling Stone*, July 19, 2012.

10. Ella Nilsen and Radina Gigova, "World Still Way Off Track on Goal to Keep Global Warming Below Dangerous Threshold, UN says," *CNN*, October 26, 2022.

11. "Greenhouse Gases Continued to Increase Rapidly in 2022," *National Oceanic and Atmospheric Administration*, April 5, 2023.

12. Chris Mooney, Juliet Eilperin, Desmond Butler, John Muyskens, Anu Narayanswamy and Naema Ahmed, "Countries' Climate Pledges Built on Flawed Data, Post Investigation Finds," *Washington Post*, November 7, 2021.

13. Hewitt Crane, Edwin Kinderman, and Ripudaman Malhotra, *A Cubic Mile of Oil: Realities and Options for Averting the Looming Global Energy Crisis* (New York: Oxford University Press, 2010).

14. "Wind and Solar Generated 10% of Global Electricity in 2021: A World First," World Economic Forum, April 8, 2022.

15. *Crash Course*, film presented by Chris Martenson (Bernardston, MA: Searchlight Films, 2009).

16. *Money as Debt*, film directed by Paul Gringon (Canada: Moonfire Studios, 2006).

17. According to usdebtclock.org.

18. Sean Ross, "Financial Services: Sizing the Sector in the Global Economy," *Investopedia*, September 30, 2021.

19. "Sources of Greenhouse Gas Emissions," United States Environmental Protection Agency, accessed September 4, 2023.

20. Heinberg, *Peak Everything*, 47–65. See also: *The Power of Community: How Cuba Survived Peak Oil*, film directed by Faith Morgan (Yellow Springs, OH: Arthur Morgan Institute for Community Solutions, 2006).

21. "2017 Census of Agriculture Data Now Available," U.S. Department of Agriculture, April 11, 2019.

22. *The Work That Reconnects: Training DVD*, presented by Joanna Macy (Gabriola Island, BC: New Society, 2006).

23. "WHO Coronavirus (COVID-19) Dashboard," World Health Organization, accessed September 4, 2023.

24. Rebecca Solnit, *A Paradise Built in Hell: The Extraordinary Communities That Arise in Disaster* (United States: Penguin Books, 2010).

25. John Gramlich, "Mental Health and the Pandemic: What U.S. Surveys Have Found," Pew Research Center, March 2, 2023.

Chapter 7: The Power of Vision

1. King James Version.
2. M. King Hubbert was a petroleum geologist who rose to notoriety when he correctly predicted that US oil production would peak around 1970.
3. Rob Hopkins, *The Transition Handbook: From Oil Dependency to Local Resilience* (England: Green Books, 2008), 93.
4. See John F. Helliwell, Richard Layard, Jeffrey D. Sachs, Jan-Emmanuel De Neve, Lara B. Aknin, and Shun Wang, *2023 World Happiness Report* (New York: Sustainable Development Solutions Network, 2023). Denmark was ranked #2 and Costa Rica was ranked #23 out of 137 countries. Bhutan was not included in this year's results.
5. I strongly encourage anyone interested in diving deeper into this subject to read Rob Hopkins, *From What Is to What If: Unleashing the Power of the Imagination to Create the Future We Want* (White River Junction, VT: Chelsea Green, 2019).
6. Hopkins, *The Transition Handbook*, 213.
7. David Holmgren, *Future Scenarios: How Communities Can Adapt to Peak Oil and Climate Change* (White River Junction, VT: Chelsea Green, 2009).
8. *An Inconvenient Truth*, film presented by Al Gore (United States: Lawrence Bender Productions and Participant Productions, 2006).
9. John Michael Greer, *The Ecotechnic Future: Envisioning a Post-Peak World* (Gabriola Island, BC: New Society, 2009).
10. Movement Generation, *From Banks and Tanks to Cooperation and Caring*, 3.
11. Kate Raworth, *Doughnut Economics: 7 Ways to Think Like a 21st Century Economist* (White River Junction, VT: Chelsea Green, 2017).
12. *A Message from the Future*, film presented by Alexandria Ocasio-Cortez and illustrated by Molly Crabapple (United States: The Intercept and Naomi Klein, 2019).
13. Movement Generation, *From Banks and Tanks to Cooperation and Caring*, 9.

Chapter 8: Inner Transition

1. Chögyam Trungpa, *Shambhala: The Sacred Path of the Warrior* (Boston: Shambhala Publications, 1984), 108–109.
2. *The History of the Inner in Transition*, video presented by Hilary Prentice and Sophy Banks (England: Transition Network, 2015).
3. Ken Wilber, *A Theory of Everything: An Integral Vision for Business, Politics, Science, and Spirituality* (United States: Shambhala Publications, 2000).

4. For a more complete description of the Three Yanas, see Chögyam Trungpa, *The Profound Treasury of the Ocean of Dharma, Volumes 1–3* (United States: Shambhala Publications, 2013).

5. For more on the Six Paramitas, see Chögyam Trungpa, *Meditation in Action* (Berkeley: Shambhala Publications, 1969).

6. "Ask Yourself What Makes You Come Alive, and Go Do That, Because What the World Needs Is People Who Have Come Alive," *Quote Investigator*, July 9, 2021.

7. *The Power of Myth*, documentary presented by Joseph Campbell and Bill Moyers (United States: Public Broadcasting Service, 1988).

8. Rainer Maria Rilke, *Letters to a Young Poet*, trans. by Stephen Mitchell (New York: Vintage Books, 1986), 6.

Chapter 9: Healthy Groups

1. "Never Doubt That a Small Group of Thoughtful, Committed Citizens Can Change the World; Indeed, It's the Only Thing That Ever Has," *Quote Investigator*, November 12, 2017.

2. Codified by Bruce Tuckman, a psychological researcher specializing in group dynamics, in 1965.

3. What constitutes normal and acceptable ways of working together can vary from culture to culture. I've found Tema Okun's list of the fifteen characteristics of "White Supremacy Culture" to be a particularly valuable tool for reflecting on my own biases.

4. There are different variations on what SMART stands for, but I like this one the best.

5. The foundational text of NVC is Marshall B. Rosenberg, *Nonviolent Communication: A Language of Life* (Encinitas, CA: PuddleDancer Press, 2003).

6. For those wanting to learn more about how to start a nonprofit organization in the US, I recommend Peri Pakroo, *Starting & Building a Nonprofit: A Practical Guide* (Berkeley: NOLO, 2021) and Anthony Mancuso, *How to Form a Nonprofit Corporation: A Step-by-Step Guide to Forming a 501(c)(3) Nonprofit in Any State* (Berkeley: NOLO, 2017).

7. Asher Miller and Rob Hopkins, *Climate After Growth: Why Environmentalists Must Embrace Post-Growth Economics and Community Resilience* (United States and England: Post Carbon Institute and Transition Network, 2013), 21.

8. Rob Hopkins, "Doria Robinson on Scaling up Community Resilience in the Shadow of Chevron," *Transition Network*, January 7, 2014.

9. Brian J. Robertson, *Organization at the Leading Edge: Introducing Holacracy* (United States: HolacracyOne, 2007).

10. I originally learned about decision-making by consent as part of Sociocracy for All's 2017 Sociocracy Leadership Training.

11. Codified by David A. Kolb, an educational theorist, in 1984.
12. The Transition Healthcheck is available as a free download on Transition Network's website.

Chapter 10: Community Engagement

1. From his 1967 "Christmas Eve Sermon on Peace."
2. Everett M. Rogers, *Diffusion of Innovations* (New York: Simon & Schuster, 1962).
3. *How to Start a Movement*, presented by Derek Sivers (Long Beach, CA: TED, 2010).
4. David Robson, "The '3.5% rule': How a Small Minority Can Change the World," *BBC*, May 13, 2019.
5. Damon Centola, Joshua Becker, Devon Brackbill, and Andrea Baronchelli, "Experimental Evidence for Tipping Points in Social Convention," *Science*, 360(6393), June 8, 2018: 1116-1119.
6. Carlo C. DiClemente, *Addiction and Change: How Addictions Develop and Addicted People Recover* (New York: Guilford Press, 2006).
7. See Juanita Brown with David Issacs and the World Cafe Community, *The World Cafe: Shaping Our Futures Through Conversations That Matter* (San Francisco: Berrett-Koehler, 2005).
8. For an even deeper dive into the fascinating Zen-like philosophy behind Open Space, read Harrison Owen, *Open Space Technology: A User's Guide* (San Francisco: Berrett-Koehler, 2008).
9. Tina's own description of her Big List activity, which is different than mine, is currently available on Transition Network's website.
10. "Tool: The Collaboration Spectrum," Tamarack Institute, 2017.
11. Van Jones, *The Green Collar Economy: How One Solution Can Fix Our Two Biggest Problems* (New York: Harper-Collins, 2008), 50–51.
12. Ibid., 55.
13. Don Edward Beck and Christopher C. Cowan, *Spiral Dynamics: Mastering Values, Leadership, and Change* (Malden, MA: Blackwell, 1996).
14. Ken Wilber, *A Theory of Everything: An Integral Vision for Business, Politics, Science and Spirituality* (United States: Shambhala Publications, 2000).
15. Another classic Rob Hopkins-ism.
16. Beck and Cowan, *Spiral Dynamics*, 146.

Chapter 11: Practical Projects

1. According to *Wikipedia*, Raymond Williams was a Welsh writer, academic, novelist, and critic. It's unclear where this quote came from, but it's all over the internet.
2. For those who are unfamiliar, Community Supported Agriculture (CSA) is a mutually beneficial partnership between a farm and its customers. Customers

provide a lump sum at the beginning of each growing season in return for a weekly share of the harvest. The farm receives an infusion of cash when it's needed most, and the customer benefits from a lower overall cost.

3. The program I'm most familiar with is Feeding Florida's Fresh Access Bucks, which doubles the value of SNAP benefits when they're used to purchase Florida produce at Florida farmers' markets.

4. This is typically referred to as the "Local Economic Multiplier Effect."

5. According to Feeding Florida's 2021 *Map the Meal Gap* survey.

6. Laura Schumm, "America's Patriotic Victory Gardens," *History*, September 1, 2018.

7. McAllister and Hall, "Transition Milwaukee and the Victory Garden Initiative," in 10 *Stories of Transition in the US*, 45–51.

8. According to repaircafe.org.

9. McAllister and Hall, "The Spread of Repair Cafes," in 10 *Stories of Transition in the US*, 20–23.

10. Cahn, a civil rights lawyer, is widely credited as the founder of the time banking movement. See Edgar S. Cahn, *No More Throw-Away People: The Co-Production Imperative* (Washington DC: Essential Books, 2000).

11. McAllister and Hall, "The Evolution of Transition Town Media," in 10 *Stories of Transition in the US*, 28–32, and Sari Steuber, "Solarize Greater Media Wrap-up," Transition Town Greater Media, November 3, 2016.

12. McAllister and Hall, "Building Community with Transition Streets," in 10 *Stories of Transition in the US*, 52–60.

13. Available at transitionstreets.org.

14. Available at readytogether.net.

15. Rob Hopkins, "A Dazzlingly Delicious Taste of the Future in Liége," *Imagination Taking Power*, March 26, 2018.

16. Rob Hopkins, "The Rise of Community Energy," in 21 *Stories of Transition: How a Movement of Communities Is Coming Together to Reimagine and Rebuild Our World* (England: Transition Network, 2015), 18–21.

17. Hopkins, "The Rise of Transition Currencies," in 21 *Stories of Transition*, 31–36.

18. Asher Miller and Rob Hopkins, *Climate After Growth: Why Environmentalists Must Embrace Post-Growth Economics and Community Resilience* (United States and England: Post Carbon Institute and Transition Network, 2013), 17.

19. McAllister and Hall, "Local 20/20's Local Investing Opportunities Network," in 10 *Stories of Transition in the US*, 39–44.

20. Emily Nonko, "An Indigenous Community Land Trust Is Creating Housing Through #LandBack," *Next City*, March 23, 2023.

21. You can watch an inspiring short video, with 3-D animated renderings of

the Atmos Totnes project, on the Totnes Community Development Society's homepage.

22. Both *In Transition 1.0: From Oil Dependence to Local Resilience*, film directed by Emma Goude (England: Transition Network, 2009) and *In Transition 2.0: A Story of Resilience and Hope in Extraordinary Times*, film directed by Emma Goude (England: Transition Network, 2012) are available to watch free online.

23. This plan is simply called *Ungersheim Village en Transition*. Its subtitle is "C'est en marchant que l'on trouve le chemin," which translates to "We make our path by walking."

Chapter 12: Part of a Movement

1. adrienne maree brown, *Emergent Strategy: Shaping Change, Changing Worlds* (Chico, CA: AK Press, 2017), 46.

2. Benjamin Ryan, "These Days, It's Not About the Polar Bears," *New York Times*, May 12, 2019.

3. These figures come from my own research and analysis of historical records kept by Transition US.

4. Rob Hopkins, *The Transition Handbook: From Oil Dependency to Local Resilience* (England: Green Books, 2008), 10.

5. Chad Otar, "What Percentage of Small Businesses Fail—And How Can You Avoid Being One of Them?" *Forbes*, October 25, 2018.

6. Bill Moyer, *The Movement Action Plan: A Strategic Framework Describing the Eight Stages of Successful Social Movements* (Cambridge, MA: Movement for a New Society, 1987).

7. Trapese Collective, "The Rocky Road to a Real Transition: The Transition Towns Movement and What It Means for Social Change," *The Commoner*, 13 (Winter 2009), 141–167.

8. Ellen Sciales, "The Civilian Climate Corps (CCC), Explained," Sunrise Movement, April 20, 2021.

9. *Blessed Unrest: How the Largest Movement in the World Came into Being and Why No One Saw It Coming*, presented by Paul Hawken (San Rafael, CA: Bioneers, 2007).

10. According to the *Wikipedia* entry for Wiser.org.

11. I'd especially recommend checking out PCI's Think Resilience online course and *What Could Possibly Go Right?* podcast.

Chapter 13: Conclusion

1. Margaret Wheatley, *Who Do We Choose to Be? Facing Reality, Claiming Leadership, Restoring Sanity* (Oakland, CA: Berrett-Koehler, 2017), 8.

2. *Journey of the Universe: An Epic Story of Cosmic, Earth, and Human Transformation,* presented by Brian Swimme (United States: KQED, 2011).

3. James Lovelock, *Gaia: A New Look at Life on Earth* (England: Oxford University Press, 1979).

4. Apollo 10 set the record for the fastest speed of a manned spacecraft at 24,791 miles per hour. Proxima Centauri b is 4.2 light-years, or 24.7 trillion miles, away from Earth.

5. Rob Hopkins, "What Did Sisyphus Dream Of?" *Imagination Taking Power*, March 4, 2020.

6. As quoted in Naomi Klein, *The Shock Doctrine: The Rise of Disaster Capitalism* (Toronto, ON: Knopf, 2007).

7. Kuhn coined the term "paradigm shift" in his 1962 book, *The Structure of Scientific Revolutions*.

8. William Butler Yeats, "The Second Coming," in *The Collected Poems of W. B. Yeats* (United States: Scribner Books, 1996).

9. Joanna Macy and Molly Young Brown, *Coming Back to Life: Practices to Reconnect Our Lives, Our World* (Gabriola Island, BC: New Society, 1998), 171–172.

10. Sharon Astyk, "The Theory of Anyway," Resilience.org, January 25, 2007.

11. Joel Pett, *USA Today*, December 7, 2009.

12. "We are the ones we've been waiting for" is a line from an anonymous poem called "A Hopi Elder Speaks."

Bibliography

Alexander, Christopher, Sara Ishikawa, and Murray Silverstein, with Max Jacobson, Ingrid Fiksdahl-King, and Shlomo Angel. *A Pattern Language: Towns, Buildings, Construction*. New York: Oxford University Press, 1977.

Bartlett, Al. *Arithmetic, Population and Energy: Sustainability 101*. Boulder, CO: University of Colorado, 2002.

brown, adrienne maree. *Emergent Strategy: Shaping Change, Changing Worlds*. Chico, CA: AK Press, 2017.

Brown, Juanita, with David Issacs and the World Cafe Community. *The World Cafe: Shaping Our Futures Through Conversations That Matter*. San Francisco: Berrett-Koehler, 2005.

Cahn, Edgar S. *No More Throw-Away People: The Co-Production Imperative*. Washington DC: Essential Books, 2000.

Campbell, Joseph. *The Hero with a Thousand Faces*. New York: Bollingen Foundation, 1949.

Campbell, Joseph, and Bill Moyer. *The Power of Myth*. Documentary. United States: Public Broadcasting Service, 1988.

Capra, Fritjof. *The Web of Life: A New Scientific Understanding of Living Systems*. New York: Anchor Books, 1997.

DiClemente, Carlo C. *Addiction and Change: How Addictions Develop and Addicted People Recover*. New York: Guilford Press, 2006.

Gandhi, M. K. *An Autobiography or The Story of My Experiments with Truth*. Translated by Mahadev Desai. India: Navajivan Publishing House, 1968.

Gore, Al. *An Inconvenient Truth*. Film. United States: Lawrence Bender Productions and Participant Productions, 2006.

Goude, Emma. *In Transition 1.0: From Oil Dependence to Local Resilience*. Film. England: Transition Network, 2009.

Goude, Emma. *In Transition 2.0: A Story of Resilience and Hope in Extraordinary Times*. Film. England: Transition Network, 2012.

Greene, Gregory. *The End of Suburbia*. Film. Canada: The Electric Wallpaper Co, 2004.

Greer, John Michael. *The Ecotechnic Future: Envisioning a Post-Peak World*. Gabriola Island, BC: New Society, 2009.

Gringon, Paul. *Money as Debt*. Film. Canada: Moonfire Studios, 2006.

Heinberg, Richard. *Peak Everything: Waking Up to the Century of Declines*. Gabriola Island, BC: New Society, 2010.

Hemenway, Toby. *Gaia's Garden: A Guide to Home-Scale Permaculture*. White River Junction, VT: Chelsea Green, 2000.

Hopkins, Rob. *From What Is to What If: Unleashing the Power of the Imagination to Create the Future We Want*. White River Junction, VT: Chelsea Green, 2019.

Hopkins, Rob. *The Transition Companion: Making Your Community More Resilient in Uncertain Times*. White River Junction, VT: Chelsea Green, 2011.

Hopkins, Rob. *The Transition Handbook: From Oil Dependency to Local Resilience*. England: Green Books, 2008.

Hopkins, Rob. *21 Stories of Transition: How a Movement of Communities Is Coming Together to Reimagine and Rebuild Our World*. England: Transition Network, 2015.

Jones, Van. *The Green Collar Economy: How One Solution Can Fix Our Two Biggest Problems*. New York: Harper-Collins, 2008.

Joyce, James. *Ulysses*. Paris: Shakespeare and Company, 1922.

Kinsale Further Education College Students and Rob Hopkins. *Kinsale 2021: An Energy Descent Action Plan*. Ireland: Kinsale Further Education College, 2005.

Klein, Naomi. *The Shock Doctrine: The Rise of Disaster Capitalism*. Toronto, ON: Knopf, 2007.

Kunstler, James Howard. *The Long Emergency: Surviving the End of Oil, Climate Change, and Other Converging Catastrophes of the Twenty-First Century*. New York: Grove Press, 2006.

Lovelock, James. *Gaia: A New Look at Life on Earth*. England: Oxford University Press, 1979.

Macy, Joanna. *The Work That Reconnects: Training DVD*. Gabriola Island, BC: New Society, 2006.

Macy, Joanna, and Molly Young Brown. *Coming Back to Life: Practices to Reconnect Our Lives, Our World*. Gabriola Island, BC: New Society, 1998.

Mancuso, Anthony. *How to Form a Nonprofit Corporation: A Step-by-Step Guide to Forming a 501(c)(3) Nonprofit in Any State*. United States: NOLO, 2017.

Martenson, Chris. *Crash Course*. Film. Bernardston, MA: Searchlight Films, 2009.

Meadows, Donella H, Dennis L. Meadows, Jørgen Randers, and William W. Behrens III. *The Limits to Growth: A Report for the Club of Rome's Project on the Predicament of Mankind*. United States: Potomac Associates, 1972.

McAllister, Steve, and Don Hall. *10 Stories of Transition in the US: Inspiring Examples of Community Resilience-Building*. Sebastopol, CA: Transition US, 2019.

Miller, Asher, and Rob Hopkins. *Climate After Growth: Why Environmentalists Must Embrace Post-Growth Economics and Community Resilience*. United States and England: Post Carbon Institute and Transition Network, 2013.

Morgan, Faith. *The Power of Community: How Cuba Survived Peak Oil*. Film. Yellow Springs, OH: Arthur Morgan Institute for Community Solutions, 2006.

Movement Generation Justice & Ecology Project. *From Banks and Tanks to Cooperation and Caring: A Strategic Framework for a Just Transition*. Berkeley, CA: Movement Generation Justice & Ecology Project, 2017.

Moyer, Bill. *The Movement Action Plan: A Strategic Framework Describing the Eight Stages of Successful Social Movements*. Cambridge, MA: Movement for a New Society, 1987.

Owen, Harrison. *Open Space Technology: A User's Guide*. San Francisco: Berrett-Koehler, 2008.

Pakroo, Peri. *Starting & Building a Nonprofit: A Practical Guide*. United States: NOLO, 2021.

Plotkin, Bill. *Wild Mind: A Field Guide to the Human Psyche*. Novato, CA: New World Library, 2013.

Raworth, Kate. *Doughnut Economics: 7 Ways to Think Like a 21st Century Economist*. White River Junction, VT: Chelsea Green, 2017.

Rilke, Rainer Maria. *Letters to a Young Poet*. Translated by Stephen Mitchell. New York: Vintage Books, 1986.

Robertson, Brian J. *Organization at the Leading Edge: Introducing Holacracy*. United States: HolacracyOne, 2007.

Rogers, Everett M. *Diffusion of Innovations, Fifth Edition*. New York: Simon & Schuster, 1962.

Rosenberg, Marshall B. *Nonviolent Communication: A Language of Life*. Encinitas, CA: PuddleDancer Press, 2003.

Sagan, Carl. *Cosmos*. Film. United States: Public Broadcasting Service, 1980.

Scharmer, C. Otto. *Theory U: Leading from the Future as It Emerges*. San Francisco: Berrett-Koehler, 2009.

Senge, Peter, C. Otto Scharmer, Joseph Jaworski, and Betty Sue Flowers. *Presence: An Exploration of Profound Change in People, Organizations, and Society*. New York: Doubleday, 2005.

Solnit, Rebecca. *A Paradise Built in Hell: The Extraordinary Communities That Arise in Disaster*. United States: Penguin Books, 2010.

Swimme, Brian. *Journey of the Universe: An Epic Story of Cosmic, Earth, and Human Transformation*. Documentary. California: KQED, 2011.

Swimme, Brian, and Thomas Berry. *The Universe Story: From the Primordial Flaring Forth to the Ecozoic Era*. New York: Harper Collins, 1992.

Thoreau, Henry D. *Walden; or, Life in the Woods*. Boston: Ticknor and Fields, 1854.

Transition Network. *The Essential Guide to Doing Transition: Getting Transition Started in Your Street, Community, Town, or Organization*. England: Transition Network, 2016.

Transition Town Totnes, with Jacqui Hodgson and Rob Hopkins. *Transition in Action: Totnes and District 2030, An Energy Descent Action Plan*. England: Green Books, 2010.

Trungpa, Chögyam. *Meditation in Action*. Berkeley: Shambhala, 1969.

Trungpa, Chögyam. *The Profound Treasury of the Ocean of Dharma, Volumes 1–3*. United States: Shambhala, 2013.

Trungpa, Chögyam. *Shambhala: The Sacred Path of the Warrior*. Boston: Shambhala, 1984.

Wheatley, Margaret. *Leadership and the New Science: Discovering Order in a Chaotic World*. Oakland, CA: Berrett-Koehler, 2006.

Wheatley, Margaret, *Who Do We Choose to Be? Facing Reality, Claiming Leadership, Restoring Sanity*. Oakland, CA: Berrett-Koehler, 2017.

Wilber, Ken. *A Theory of Everything: An Integral Vision for Business, Politics, Science, and Spirituality*. Boston: Shambhala, 2000.

Index

Page numbers in *italics* indicate figures and tables.

About the Author

DON HALL has served in a variety of capacities throughout the international Transition Towns Movement over the past 15 years, first as Education & Outreach Coordinator for Transition Colorado, then as Founder and Executive Director of Transition Sarasota (Florida), and Executive Director of Transition US. He is currently Training Coordinator for the international Transition Network. Don holds a master's degree in Environmental Leadership from Naropa University, a certification in Permaculture Design from the Central Rocky Mountain Permaculture Institute, and regularly teaches on a wide variety of topics including leadership development, community organizing, effective collaboration, and local food systems. In 2019, Don edited and published *10 Stories of Transition in the US: Inspiring Examples of Community Resilience-Building*. He currently lives in Boulder, Colorado and manages the website evolutionarychange.org.

ABOUT NEW SOCIETY PUBLISHERS

New Society Publishers is an activist, solutions-oriented publisher focused on publishing books to build a more just and sustainable future. Our books offer tips, tools, and insights from leading experts in a wide range of areas.

We're proud to hold to the highest environmental and social standards of any publisher in North America. When you buy New Society books, you are part of the solution!

At New Society Publishers, we care deeply about *what* we publish—but also about *how* we do business.

- This book is printed on 100% **post-consumer recycled paper**, processed chlorine-free, with low-VOC vegetable-based inks (since 2002)

- Our corporate structure is an innovative employee shareholder agreement, so we're one-third employee-owned (since 2015)

- We've created a Statement of Ethics (2021). The intent of this Statement is to act as a framework to guide our actions and facilitate feedback for continuous improvement of our work

- We're carbon-neutral (since 2006)

- We're certified as a B Corporation (since 2016)

- We're Signatories to the UN's Sustainable Development Goals (SDG) Publishers Compact (2020–2030, the Decade of Action)

To download our full catalog, sign up for our quarterly newsletter, and to learn more about New Society Publishers, please visit newsociety.com.

ENVIRONMENTAL BENEFITS STATEMENT

New Society Publishers saved the following resources by printing the pages of this book on chlorine free paper made with 100% post-consumer waste.

TREES	WATER	ENERGY	SOLID WASTE	GREENHOUSE GASES
39	3,000	16	140	16,600
FULLY GROWN	GALLONS	MILLION BTUs	POUNDS	POUNDS

Environmental impact estimates were made using the Environmental Paper Network Paper Calculator 4.0. For more information visit www.papercalculator.org